OPEN FELL HIDDEN DALE

Photographs by John & Eliza Forder
Text by Arthur Raistrick

Best Wishes,

John & Eliza Forder

We would like to dedicate this book to
the people of the Dales who have
shown us so much kindness and
patience while we photographed.
We would also like to thank Northern
Arts for their help in past years, and
Richard David for his constant support
and guidance.

ISBN 0 9504730 9 **X**

Published by
Frank Peters Publishing Ltd.
Kendal, Cumbria

Printed by
Frank Peters Printers Ltd.
Kendal, Cumbria

Designed by
Ram Design Associates Ltd.
Kendal, Cumbria

THE PHOTOGRAPHS

Barbondale — looking along the line of the Dent Fault
East Gill Foss at Kisdon, Swaledale
Chapel-le-Dale with its glaciated limestone scars
Dent Head Viaduct and Dentdale
Langstrothdale — upper Wharfedale
A drove-road on Combe Fell
Kitty Gill bringing in the 'eldin'
Hardrow Force
Rowten Pot's 200′ shaft
Gunnerside Gill
George Winn
Erosion channels in Coverdale
The River Dee
Pendragon Castle and Wild Boar Fell
Swaledale from the Buttertubs Pass
Thwaite, Swaledale — a Norse settlement
Jim and Ivy Mason from Barras House, Gawthrop
Herbert and Ennis Bentham on their way to mark the tup
Scotchergill Farm
Jim Taylor taking his cows to be milked
Alan Mattinson converts a Dales barn
Mily Taylor and John Murdoch at dominoes in the Sun Inn, Dent
Main Street, Dent
Ingleborough and limestone pavement
The Main Chamber of Gaping Gill — Britain's largest known cavern
Kilnsey Crag from Conistone — the flat foreground was a glacial lake
White Scar Cave
Herb Robert growing on a stone wall
The Buttertubs
Old Cote Moor across Littondale
Feeding Swaledale sheep above Artengill Viaduct
Bob Johnson and his crooks
A crook carved from a Swaledale tup's horn
Askrigg Village and Addleborough
Denys Stark, the proprietor
Ivy Bentham, East Banks Farm
A Long House near Appersett
Ingleton Quarry — working in Yorkshire's oldest rock
Pete Moorby and Jo Hartley repair the Chapel roof using stone slates
Shaw Beck — remains of a lead-mining hamlet
Elizabeth and Thomas Gardner at Banklands Farm
Dent Village under Rise Hill
Deepdale Beck at Mill Bridge
Ted Sedgwick from New Closes, Cowgill
The Howgill Fells from Deepdale
A traditional hay meadow in Swaledale
Getting the hay in — Deepdale
Robert Mason rounding up the tups with his dog 'Leo'
Tug of war — Gala Day
Malham Cove
Malham Tarn with Great Crested Grebe
The Shores of Malham Tarn, with alder, birch and 'bog baby warning'
Watlowes at Malham — a dry valley
Alum Pot as seen from the Long Churn Cave System
Grotto in Gavel Pot
Ribblehead Viaduct and Batty Moss
Aysgarth — The Middle Falls
The Coal Road winds across the fell to Garsdale
Stephen and Gordon Gardner with sheep-clippers
'Tizza' Middleton
Wood Anemones in a gryke

Lockingarth Falls, Deepdale
Icicle detail
Jo and Phyllis Woof dipping sheep at Cautley
A pack-horse track cuts across Greenhow Hill
Hubberholme Church
School children — West Burton
Tommy Capstick and Harold Goad having a 'biting on'
Colt Park — relict ash-wood
Janet's Foss — The Fairy's Cave
The Roof Tunnel in Kingsdale Master Cave
Yew Cogar Scars rise sharply above Cowside Beck
A cascade on Deepdale Beck cuts through the Yoredale Strata
Main Stream Passage, Lancaster Hole
Swaledale
Mist rising from the Keld
'Topping' a wall in Kingsdale
Richard Charnley at Hawes Market
Brushing the sheeps' faces ready for the Mule Gimmer Sale
Beth of Dent
Formations in Cross Fell Cave
Gordale Scar
Gordale Beck — downstream from Janet's Foss
Jervaulx Abbey
Jervaulx Abbey — detail of one of its numerous stone arches
Alum Pot 240 'below the surface
Dentdale and Middleton Fell
Martin Cragg with the muck-spreader
Ben Munro's Bicycle Shop
Mr and Mrs Baines at Backstone Gill, Dentdale
Douglas Hartley catching the wayward lamb
Pen-y-ghent — early morning
Willie Bentham

CONTENTS

Introduction: 11

Map of the Dales   12

PART 1: THE LAND

The Making of the Landscape   13

The Karst   15

The Peaks   16

The Moorlands   18

The Dales   20

PART 2: THE PEOPLE

Stone and Bronze   23

The Coming of the Celts   25

Angles, Danes, Norsemen   27

Norman Conquest   30

The Monasteries   34

Widening Horizons   36

Industrial Revolution   40

The Spirit of the Dales   44

THE PHOTOGRAPHS   47

Index   142

INTRODUCTION

The Yorkshire Dales lie in the central part of the Pennine range.

The area is roughly defined by the market towns of Richmond, Pateley Bridge and Ilkley in the east, and Kirkby Lonsdale and Kirkby Stephen in the west. It is essentially a plateau of heather and grass clad moors, with many of the peaks rising above this to over 2000 feet. The plateau is dissected by the valleys of seven rivers into which flow hundreds of tributaries that form gorges, backs and waterfalls — all characteristics of the Dales.

In the two environments, moor and valley, life and human activities differ widely. In the dales the daily occupations of the dairy farm, and the cultural and recreational life of the community have imposed a rich human pattern. The 'tops', or fells, are at present largely a place of solitude except for the shepherd and game-keeper, the sheep and the birds, and in recent years a growing number of active visitors who are now discovering their attractions.

Within the area too, there is a third region to be taken into account, though it usually remains unseen. The limestones of the Dales are honeycombed with pot-holes, underground streams and caves of vast size, which appear ever more extensive as cavers continue their systematic explorations.

The geology, topography and physical history of the Dales have created a landscape with a basic uniformity, but there is almost infinite variety of detail that allows each dale to sustain its own unmistakeable identity. An important line of demarcation is the broad belt of the highest peaks and moors — the north to south watershed of the Pennines — from which dales extend either side. The rivers to the east are long and eventually join the Ouse and then the Humber before reaching the North Sea. Their broader valleys — Wharfedale, Wensleydale and Swaledale — have rich dairy farms, villages and a scattering of castles and abbeys. The rivers to the west have a shorter journey to the Irish Sea and the valleys of the Clough (Garsdale), Dee (Dentdale), Rawthey and the Lune are narrower, with affinity to the Lake District, whose geology and historic traditions they in part share. The western district is characterised by hamlets, dispersed upland homes and sheep-farming. The watershed is not only a topographic divide, but has ethnic significance too: the settlements to the west were predominantly Norse, and those to the east, Anglo-Danish. Dialect, tradition, legend and many details of the way of life reflect these differing backgrounds.

The landscape of the Dales has provided a home for humans who have known it intimately, called it theirs, mapped its features and loved it in varying degrees during ten millenia. It is only during a little more than the last millennium that the area has been defined and named as Yorkshire, and its inhabitants have slowly consolidated the loyalties by which they recognise themselves as Yorkshiremen and Dalesmen. The claim to be such is proudly shared by the people of the area, for although those in particular dales may be distinguished by slight differences, they all share a basic character. We can better understand and appreciate that character the more we know of the physical features that have been the scene of the long chain of human life and endeavour in the past. We are only the latest link in the chain. It is our privilige and responsibility to enjoy and use what our predecessors helped to create, and in our turn to pass it on the next generation.

This book is an effort to illuminate verbally and visually the nature and spirit of the Dales environment, and the society that lives within it. The text describes the geological and historical processes through which the land and people evolved to reach their present condition. The photographs record that condition.

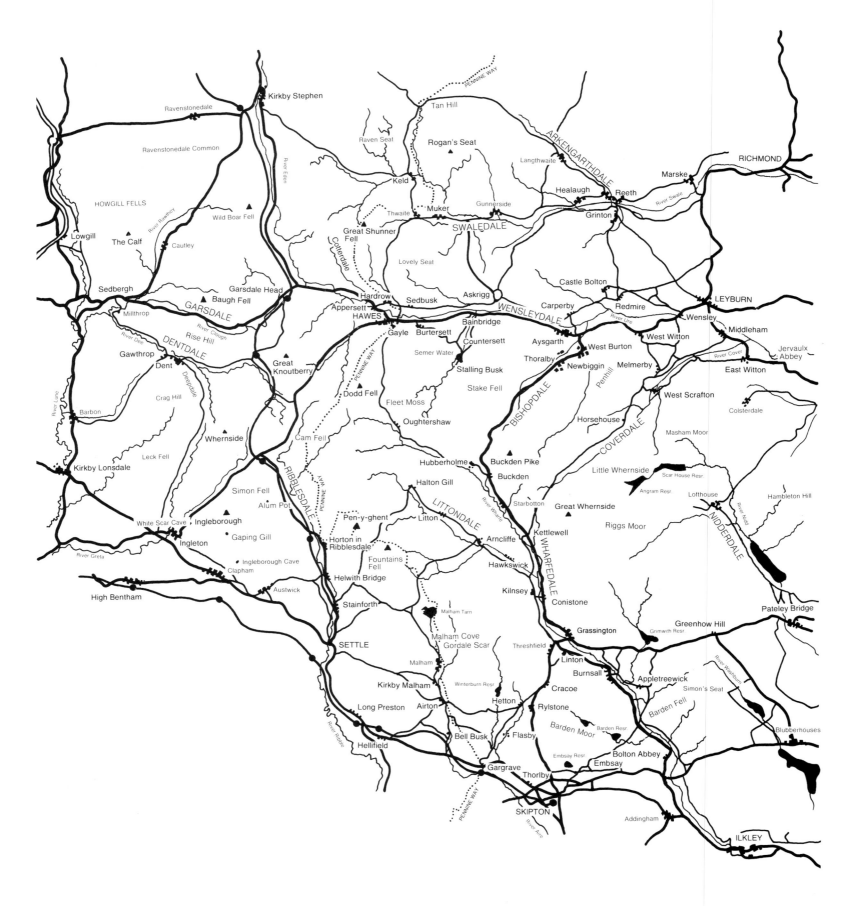

PART 1: THE LAND
The Making of the Landscape

The landscape and scenery of this portion of the Pennines are the product of sculpting by the normal tools of erosion, ice, water and climate, which during the time of the later geological strata, cut into the surface formed by the ancient Pennine Uplift. The geology is in general terms simple and is clearly displayed to those who have the incentive to look, eyes to observe, and patience to store up impressions and experiences. A controlled and informed imagination will find itself confronted and stretched by a scene, the components of which originated some hundreds of millions of years ago. As we admire the rocks over which the Ingleton waterfalls tumble in such splendour, we are looking at consolidated deposits laid down in a sea that existed in the very early ages of the geological story, when the evolution of life on earth was in its most primitive stages. Turning to look at the Howgill Fells, we see the products of a vastly younger sea, but one still incredibly ancient, its age to be stated in millions of years at a time when life was still only represented by marine creatures without backbones, the invertebrates.

Let us begin at a time when the great volcanoes, which poured out the thousands of feet thickness of lava from which in part the mountains of the Lake District are carved, were still a recent geological event. Evolution was only approaching the great step that brought forth the first primitive fishes. Several million years were to pass while true fishes were added to the world of living creatures and the silts of the Howgill rocks accumulated. There followed a period when much of the region was wide-spreading hot desert, with other seas from which plants and vertebrates escaped to people the land for the first time. This was the Devonian period of the geologist.

In the latter part of this period great movements of the earth's crust forced up a mountain chain very much higher than the Pennines now are, in which the old rocks were tightly folded. Erosion attacked these folded rocks and reduced them to a very irregular approximate plain, which on subsidence became the floor of the succeeding Carboniferous sea. Geologists give this mountain-building the high-sounding but descriptive name of the 'Caledonian Orogenesis', for its greatest effect was seen in the Scottish mountains.

If your imagination has survived all these gigantic vicissitudes, you can now more restfully contemplate a long period of quiet, warm seas in which, during a few millions of years, the limestones and sandstones from which, eventually, our Dales scenery has been carved, were being laid down on a sea bed formed of the worn-down remnants of the folded mountain chain. Stand for a moment in Arcow Wood Quarry in Ribblesdale and see the beds of limestone lying nearly horizontal across the nearly vertical slates which are a part of the former mountains. At many places around the sides of Ribblesdale and Crummackdale you can observe this same unconformity and experience the thrill of spanning with one hand a gap of several hundred million years of geological history. If you go to Ingleton and along the rather precarious path that creeps behind the water of Thornton Force, you can span an even longer gap.

For a very long time the temperate waters of the Carboniferous sea teemed with countless myriads of almost microscopic plants and animals, the diatoms and foraminifera. Bivalve shellfish swarmed; in some environments corals were abundant, in others crinoids, mistakenly called 'sea lilies'. There were fishes of forms now extinct, and many varieties of sponges. The skeletons of all these creatures, which piled up as chalky mud, formed the hundreds of feet of the Carboniferous Limestone and can still be recognised as fossils. In some layers the fossils are perfectly preserved and we can see and handle them or just admire them as patterns in the polished rocks such as the 'Dent Marble'.

Above the Carboniferous limestone the succeeding thousand feet are the Yoredale Series, named by Philips in 1833 from their occurrence in Yoredale (that is Wensleydale), which takes its character from the Series' unique constitution. Climb the side of the upper valley of the Ure, and several times in your ascent you will encounter a white wall of limestone and then cross a wide gently rising shelf carpeted with a rich grassy turf. This mounts to a scree slope leading you up to the next limestone wall. Often in the scree you may see the slaty sandstone, debris from a partly concealed flagstone quarry. If a way can be found into this you will discover a maze of underground workings penetrating far into the beds just below the next limestone. The Yoredale Series are the deposits made in shallow, clear water, warm lagoons intermittently invaded by the mud and sand of rivers. Now these deposits show as the often repeated units of limestone-shale-sandstone from which our loveliest dales have been carved.

The uplift of a continental mass to the north created rivers which piled up enormous deltas across the sinking Yoredale seas and formed the thousands of feet of sandstones and shales of the Millstone Grit. On these deltas, as seas were replaced by swamps, the forests, from which our coal seams were formed, grew. Forest occasionally crept over some of the sand deposits in the Yoredales too, so that a feature of the moors that separate the dales is the abundance of collieries, at which Dalesmen have worked from the thirteenth century even to the early years of the twentieth.

There are still two major geological events that cannot be overlooked if we are to appreciate the story to be read in the rocks of the Dales. The first was another era of unrest which put an end to the quiet seas and forests of the Carboniferous period. Giant earth movements again raised a mountain chain of which the Pennines are a remnant of the foundations. Great fracturings of the uplifted rocks frame the northern part of this Pennine remnant between the rivers Aire and Tyne and cut it off from the present Vale of Eden and Howgill Fells on the west.

These fractures form the south boundary of the Tyne Valley and range across Craven creating splendid features such as Bucker Brow (now called Buck Haw Brow), Malham Cove and Gordale Scar and influencing the scenery in many minor ways. In some parts these fractures, or 'faults', represent a vertical movement of the earth for over five thousand feet. As part of the process, masses of granite were injected into the core of the rising strata. One such mass underlies the area between the Craven Faults and the wild pass of Stainmore. This forms the 'Askrigg Block' and north of it, under Teesdale, Weardale and Alston Moor, granite again gives rigidity to the 'Alston Block'. It is this rigidity that has enabled the blocks to resist later folding through many geological periods. During these later periods great thicknesses of strata covered what is now the Pennines but have since been eroded, leaving the nearly horizontal Carboniferous mass exposed and unfolded except at a few places on the western border down the Vale of Eden and Rawthey Valley. After another subsidence, for many geological ages sediments were piled into seas that covered the proto-Pennine area, only to be carried away by erosion in their turn. It was this last great erosion that re-exposed and shaped the Pennine foundations almost as we know them. The present dales, fells and mountains were formed by the rivers that we now know in their maturity.

The second great event — the last in this age-long and complex story of repeated elevation and subsidence, deposition and erosion, during the very latest phases of which primitive man began his long progress towards civilisation — was the Ice Age. This occupied the last million years, and in the thinking of some scientists has not finished yet. Ice sheets, now only remaining in shrunken Arctic remnants, extended over the northern regions.

In America the ice stretched as far south as the Great Lakes. In Europe a vast sheet covered the north-west, extending as far south as the Thames valley, the South Wales coast and in Ireland almost to the south coast. Within this area the Pennine ice field filled all the valleys and coalesced into a mass covering all but a very few of the highest summits.

The ice, moving as glaciers down the valleys and with its hundreds of feet of thickness exerting tremendous pressure, eroded and smoothed the existing landscape and removed all the soil. Sharp-cut valleys were moulded to the fine U-shape they now have, the sides steepened and the bottom broadened; strata of differing hardness were distinguished by the more effective erosion of the softer shales so that many of the fine limestone cliffs and scars were made more prominent. The eroded material was carried in and upon the ice to the lower levels. When the ice finally melted, this mixture of rock flour, pebbles, and even large boulders was dropped as boulder clay, which formed thin soils on the uplands but in the valleys was deposited along the sides as moraines and frequently, during pauses in the melting, as transverse ridges across the valley floor. These valley moraines held up the drainage of the melt water, and for a short period the Dales were a true lake district. The lakes later filled with silts and gave us the rich valley bottom land. The lateral moraines formed well-drained and firm dry routes along the valley sides and on these, tracks were easy to make and villages could be satisfactorily settled.

The ice at its maximum extent just failed to cover entirely a few of the highest peaks, so that small areas of the summits of Ingleborough and Whernside stood up as little islands above the ice. To the east of them Pen-y-ghent and Fountains Fell were also 'nunatakr', as the glacialist names these islands. Across Wharfedale, Great Whernside, Buckden Pike and Middle Tongue were again nunatakr. To the north there was thicker ice and the only prominent uncovered patches were Lovely Seat, Stang, and Water Crag. We shall return to these later, because by a near miracle a few of the alpine plants braved all the rigours of the Ice Age and survived for our present delight. No thinking person can stand by these precious plants without being awed by the wonder of their survival and contemplation of the conditions that they endured as a spot of life in an icy desert.

The Karst

In an overall view, the morphology of the whole Dales area can be seen as tripartite. In the simplest terms the area may be defined as an extensive plateau, its varying levels ranging between a thousand feet and fifteen hundred feet above sea level with minor exceptions above and below; but above the plateau there are nearly twelve peaks that rise to more than two thousand feet, and cutting down into the plateau are the deep valleys of seven main rivers with a host of tributary valleys. Of these environments the plateau offers the most variety.

The general dip of the strata of the Carboniferous from off the Askrigg Dome is gently towards the north-east, and this has had a striking effect on the nature of the upland. The moors in the east and north-east are dominated by the Millstone Grit and are peat and heather moors; in the south-west the plateau is very largely the top of the Carboniferous Limestone. This area (Craven and some of its fringes) forms the finest and largest area of karst landscape in Britain. The limestone pavements extend to hundreds of acres of bare rock, transected by an almost rectangular mesh of widened and gaping joints that require the walker to exercise considerable care and skill as he progresses along the stepping-stones of the clints. His necessary attention is liable to be constantly diverted by the fantastic weathering of the clints with their rain-sculptured shapes and surface patterns, while he cannot but be conscious of a rich flora of ferns and flowering plants inhabiting the warm and safe shelter of the wider and deeper grykes between the clints. Here, safe from any questing sheep and from all winds, he will see fine growths of the Hart's Tongue and Rigid Buckler Ferns *(Phyllitis scolopendrium* and *Dryopteris villarii)* and of the smaller and less obvious Green Spleenwort *(Asplenium viride.)* Here and there he may come across the fluffy white flowers or black berries of the Baneberry *(Actaea spicata),* a speciality of the region, while Bloody Cranesbill *(Geranium sanguineum)* is frequent. In larger grykes trees have occasionally taken root and relieve the bare extent of limestone: ash, sycamore, birch occur and, in a few special places, remnants of a juniper cover.

In places between the pavements, wherever a little water may lie in mires or calcareous flushes or on the banks of rivulets, another speciality of the region may be found. This is the Bird's-eye Primrose *(Primula farinosa),* which studs the moist earth with little grey-green rosettes of leaves and, in early June, creates drifts of mauve-pink bouquets.

The unique karst landscape has, besides its surface beauty, a whole hidden dimension. This is the underworld of caves and potholes, only a small part of which is accessible to the ordinary visitor. This world of caves was greeted by the Victorian and Edwardian traveller with horror and awe but has now become a focus of genuine wonder, intensive study, and excited exploration that can claim kinship with the great geographic explorations at least in the spirit and endurance demanded. Streams rising in the higher-lying beds of the Carboniferous usually sink underground soon after they reach the limestone, as the mildly acid water erodes the bedding planes and joints to form caves and potholes. The more or less horizontal bedding planes, that represent an interface between different depositional periods, give rise to cave passages, while the joints — at right angles to the bedding — and faults allow the water to plunge down vertical drops or 'pitches', sometimes falling several hundred feet in the process. The most famous of the open shafts is Gaping Gill, where Fell Beck falls 310 feet to the floor of the main chamber, a magnificent and awe-inspiring spectacle.

In addition to the obvious stream-sinks, water can work its way into the cracks and fissures of a bare limestone surface to give the characteristic pattern of clints and grykes of the limestone pavements. In such cases the underground percolation only becomes integrated into cave passages at some depth. Either way, a typical feature of karst scenery is the small number, or total lack, of surface streams as the drainage is substantially underground.

Although the history of cave exploration stretches back into antiquity and a few of the more obvious caves had been fairly well explored two or three hundred years ago, caving is a relatively modern pastime. Local people were essaying quite ambitious undertakings around the middle of the last century, but it appears to have been the activities of the Frenchman, M. Martel, who made the first descent of Gaping Gill in 1895, that spurred the natives to greater efforts. In the 'golden age' of cave exploration, which can be taken as the first two or three decades of the present century, the participants achieved some outstanding explorations in spite of lacking the sophisticated equipment of the modern caver. The immediate post-war years saw the opening up of several major systems, most notably the Ease Gill Cave System, at the present time the longest known cave in Britain, with over 30 miles of interconnecting passage-way. Again in the 1960's and 1970's, no doubt as the result of the widespread use of more effective protective clothing, light-weight equipment and reliable lights, a further series of spectacular discoveries was made. Exploration of 'new' caves still proceeds at the present time.

The caves themselves range from short, easy passages that can be explored with nothing more than old clothes, a torch and a pair of wellingtons, to strenuous and difficult systems involving, for example, deep shafts with waterfalls tumbling down. Indeed, part of the lure of caving is that the underground systems constitute a whole new world: a world of tunnels and canyons, rivers, and streams confined in gorge-like passages, squeezes and crawls, chambers and grottoes, cascades, and huge pitches. The low tunnels of Gaping Gill contrast with the majesty of the Main Chamber; the magnificence of the Main Stream Passage of Lancaster Hole or the beauty of the formations in Easter Grotto are better appreciated by contrast with the sombre grandeur of the old, relic tunnels long since abandoned by the river that formed them.

After travelling through the cave systems, the streams eventually emerge in one or other of the valleys or gorges surrounding the peaks. These resurgences are fewer in number than the sinks, as several streams generally unite underground to flow to one spring. Tests using dyes or salts have proved many of the connections from sink to resurgence: for example, the water falling into Gaping Gill has for long been known to emerge as the stream at Clapham Beck Head, hard by Ingleborough Cave, but it is only recently that connnecting passages have been found. Similarly water from Malham Tarn disappears at the Water Sinks, to reappear below Malham Village at the powerful Aire Head Springs, although the route through remains totally unexplored. For all those people who know the familiar peaks of Whernside, Pen-y-ghent and Ingleborough, how few realise the extent of the underground world beneath them.

The Peaks

Towering above the karst plateau a few peaks stand out not as a part of a mountain mass but as individual monuments in their own right, each standing free on its own particular pedestal. Their shapes are individual and different, recognisable from long distances away. They are a friendly presence in the background of wide scenes and an indispensable element of the skyline view in many directions. In the everyday life of the Dales they are always there, wearing their cloud-cap, made brilliant by a snow cover, brightly coloured in the sunset rays, always changing yet always the same friendly mass. To see Ingleborough from the southern fells of the Lake District is to recognise an old friend with a warmth of feeling that some of the round-topped hills further north and east may never provoke.

All these peaks have a cap of Millstone Grit, small in the south-west but rapidly growing in size to the north and east where the peaks merge into the Millstone Grit moorlands and where the limestone base is no longer visible. In the south-west the greater part of their bulk is composed of Yoredale strata and their slopes are very steep. The Yoredale limestones as well as the grit caps make cliffs and scars which give a stepped and ragged outline to the hill profile. It is these profiles that are so distinctive: Ingleborough, Pen-y-ghent, Wild Boar Fell all have their near summit cliffs and ledges. In the north and north-east the hills are largely composed of Millstone Grit which is fairly uniform in its resistance to erosion, so that smooth rounded shapes predominate and true peaks are absent. Occasional outcrops of grit provide a little more variety; Water Crag, Rogan's Seat, and a few others such as Great Shunner Fell are well identified by their great bulk. A characteristic of many of the Millstone Grit hills is the flat summit formed by a strong member of the grit series. This gives such positive shapes as those of Wild Boar Fell and Addlebrough with their ring of 'edges', and, only slightly less emphatic, the steep edges on Penhill, Shunner Fell, and many other of the high grit fells. Many of these, because of their drier, sandy soils, have provided settlement sites for early man and many such sites, both defensive and habitational, can still be seen today.

The peaks of the karst afford special habitats for many rare plants, especially where the shales in the Yoredale strata allow springs of water, the so-called 'flushes', to run. At these there is usually some accumulation of humus, with the likelihood that alpine species such as the Yellow Mountain Saxifrage *(Saxifraga aizoides)*, Purple Saxifrage *(S. oppositifolia)*, and Dovedale Moss *(S. hypnoides)* will be present. As the summits of some of these peaks were nunatakr throughout the Ice Age, some species survived there to spread later onto lower ledges. The rarest of these, Mountain Avens *(Dryas octopetala)* is found only in one or two places but at quite low altitudes. Patches of heather occur occasionally where the slope is less steep and where perhaps small areas of boulder clay remain, but the common cover of these peaks is mountain grassland, with Blue Sesleria *(Sesleria albicans)* dominant on all the limestone outcrops.

The peaks of the Millstone Grit contrast in flora as well as in shape. The poor, thin acid soils and the gentler slopes support a moorland assemblage not very different from that which is normal to the widespread moors of the plateau. The chief difference is the absence of the thick peats and the bogs with their special flora. The typical communities on the grit summits include Cloudberry *(Rubus chamaemorus)*, Crowberry *(Empetrum nigrum)*, Blaeberry *(Vaccinium myrtillus)* and, on some, *Saxifraga hypnoides*. With variations of soil and other conditions, upland grasses will invade and spread, in many places replacing the heath plants. The common grasses are Sheep's Fescue (a form of *Festuca ovina*) and the Bent Grasses *(Agrostis canina* and *A. capillaris)* both of which are valuable grazing for sheep. On the poorest soils the Mat Grass *(Nardus stricta)* and the Heath Rush *(Juncus squarresus)* are quick to colonise, and all these give the hilltops and steeper slopes a silvery cover broken here and there by the brownish purple masses of the heathers.

All the peaks of whatever composition bear a somewhat paradoxical reputation, well-loved as prominent features of the home country, watched and consulted for weather portents, but at the same time often feared and seldom climbed by the general population of the Dales. Many are the subject of ancient legends, some, like that of the Giant of Penhill, being quite frightening.

Penhill — a name of Celtic origin — is a mountain lying between Waldendale and Cotterdale, two tributaries of the Ure on the south side of Wensleydale. The legend has been elaborated into a complex and romantic story, but its elements are fairly simple. The characters are the Giant of Penhill, his wolfhound called Wolfhead, Gunda a shepherdess, the Wiseman or Hermit of Carperby and the local population, servants and tenants of the Giant. No time is assigned to the story except 'long, long ago'.

The chief wealth of the Giant lay in his vast herd of swine, in which he had one boar, a favourite above all others. Once while inspecting his flock he met Gunda with her sheep, and to satisfy his love of cruel sport he set Wolfhead to tearing the throats of Gunda's sheep. Gunda pleaded with him to call off his dog and save her sheep, for they were her family's only means of livelihood. It was in vain; struck by her beauty the Giant began to make love to her, asking her to come with him to his castle. She, however, refused all his advances and ran away into the forest. Wolfhead was sent after her and soon caught up with her, pulled her down and began worrying her. She found a big stone to hand and with it battered Wolfhead's soft muzzle. The Giant coming up to them was so furious that he battered Gunda to death with his club, then bathed the hound in her blood. When Wolfhead growled at him he took a spear and killed him.

Some time later his favourite boar was shot with an arrow. When the culprit could not be identified, the Giant called for the first-born children of all his tenants and threatened to kill them one by one until some one confessed or betrayed the guilty one. It was then that the wise man of Carperby arrived to warn him that he would never again enter his castle alive or dead. The Giant began to carry out his threat, but looking round he saw his castle burst into flames, and saw too the ghosts of Gunda and

Wolfhead approaching him. He retreated backward from them and, driven over a high precipice, disappeared and was never seen again.

On the summit of Penhill there are two extensive Iron Age (Celtic) settlements. It is possible that this story has in it fragments of Celtic mythology that may have been told round the fires of those settlements — fragments later elaborated by Norse settlers in the Dales, and further elaborated with new detail while being passed on by word of mouth through many succeeding generations. Seventy years ago the story was frequently told me by my grandmother with far more detail than is included in this summary; now it would be difficult to find anyone who remembers it.

Some peaks are skirted round their lower flanks by ancient ways, and a few are redeemed by other human connections. Folk memory retains Ingleborough as a camp and refuge, the defended fort of the Brigantes under Venutius against the Romans. The many hut circles within its defensive wall call up a vivid picture of the camp's crowded population watching the approaching Roman troops, but remaining unassailed in their mountain stronghold as the attack was switched to the great fort of Stanwick in the north-east. Ruskin, looking for the first time in awe upon Ingleborough from the head of Widdale valley, compared it with Crough Patrick in County Mayo and said "I feel [it] should be respected as a 'holy mountain'." Several of the peaks were beacons in later centuries, giving warning of imminent dangers such as invading Scots or in a nearer time bearing an important part in the preparations against the feared invasion by the French. The strength of the folk memory may be illustrated by the deep impression made upon me by the stories told to me as a very small boy by my grandfather. He had, from his grandfather, tales of carrying fuel up to, and of watching by, one of the Dales beacons when 'Bony' was the common scare.

The names of many peaks are significant of their early importance: Pen-y-ghent, Penhill, Pendle were named by the Celts in pre-Roman times; Norsemen named Shunner Fell, Lunersett, later corrupted to Lovely Seat, Rogan's Seat and many others. Forgotten stories must lie behind Wild Boar Fell, Simon Fell on Ingleborough, and many more, while Whernside reminds us of the hill's wide service as the source of querns, so necessary for domestic supplies of flour.

The Moorlands

Ask a visitor from the lowlands what makes up the Yorkshire Dales area and he would probably answer 'dales and moors'; and it is almost true that if you are not in a dale then you are on a moor. The distinction could also be made quite simply as between enclosed cultivated land and uncultivated wild. The moorlands occupy the greater part of the land over about a thousand feet above sea level and are characterised by acid and infertile soils that support much the same vegetation of heathers, sedges and mountain grasses as is found on the Millstone Grit peaks. In some parts the Purple Moor Grass *(Molinia caerulea)* is dominant, and in the wetter hollows it is joined by Cotton Grass *(Eriophorum angustifolium* and *E. vaginatum)* and *Sphagnum* mosses. Various mixtures of these vegetation types can of course be found, but all are in sharp contrast with those of the karst already described.

The moors may at times be solitary but they are never silent. To the caring listener the basic sound is that of the heather rustling in a gentle breeze. Once heard this forms a persistent ever-present background. Against it three bird cries are inseparable from the high moors: the 'go-back, go-back' of grouse, unique to them, heard nowhere but on moorland, an integral part of the daylight environment; the single, most melancholy note of the golden plover; and the cry of the curlew. Its two whistles, though shared with meadowland and the sea-shore, are as much an essential part of the moors as is the call of the grouse. Flocks of curlew invade the moorland at breeding time to make their primitive scooped nest in the heather. For the Dalesfolk for centuries past, and still perhaps for the elders of the pre-motor, pre-BBC generation, the curlew could be a supernatural haunter. Gabriel-Ratchets and the Seven Whistlers are only two of the names by which they were known. A never-to-be-forgotten experience of my youth was to be standing on a moorland path late at night, listening to the distant calls of a small flock of curlew and thinking of the Seven Whistlers. Then the cries stopped and the flock settled in the heather not far away, silent and mysterious as ghosts. This manifestation would have been full of foreboding and significance for my grandfather, who had often told me of it, and also for earlier generations of travellers.

We have lost this part of the spirit of the moors, but perhaps have exchanged it for a more aesthetic appreciation.

The karst is really an area of erosion and the uncovering of rock. Early visitors to Craven saw as one of its minor wonders large boulders of slate poised on short pedestal stems of limestone. These firmly balanced rocks, most numerous around Norber, (and one, Samson's Toe, near the well-used road from Langcliffe to Malham), were brought out of Ribblesdale on the breast of a glacier and left on the cleaned surface of the limestone when the ice melted many thousands of years ago.

These insoluble slate boulders acted as an umbrella to the patches of limestone on which they rested. Such patches were sheltered from the solvent action of the rain while all around, the limestone surface was being slowly taken away in solution. When at last a boulder topples off its pedestal we can actually see a fragment of the ice-scratched Ice Age land-surface — another of the quietly hiding secrets waiting to speak to us of the long and thrilling history of the landscape we admire.

In marked contrast with the eroded karst, the heather moorlands are areas of preservation and accumulation. In some places layers of peat twenty, thirty or even forty feet thick have accumulated, blanketing much of the moorland ground. Some of the most impressive views in the Central Pennines are the seemingly endless miles of moorland in which the dales lie hidden. The moors show a minimum of variation except as between areas of heather, grass or bog. And yet to examine their origins is to encounter a story as romantic as that of any castle, abbey or other conventional historic monument offered by the Dales.

Much of the uniqueness of the moors resides in the special quality of the peat that clothes them as the soils clothe the lowlands. In fact the commonest form taken by the peat is precisely that which is distinguished as 'blanket peat': it does indeed blanket the ground in varying thickness. Peat is unique in its preservative property, which itself is the cause of its formation. It is composed of plant remains that have accumulated in anaerobic conditions, that is in the absence of the oxygen of air and of the abundant bacteriological life that goes with it. With the production of ulmic and humic acids, decay is prevented and organic remains are preserved.

This has been romantically demonstrated by the fate of an unnamed Romano-British person, who had the misfortune to stray into a bog on the Grewelthorpe moors some time during the Roman occupation and to be completely engulfed. In 1850 his body was discovered in the course of peat cutting, and it was in a well-preserved condition. The man was fully clothed and the body intact. He wore a green cloak and an undergarment of scarlet cloth, yellow stockings and leather shoes. Local sentiment led to the body being given burial in the churchyard at Grewelthorpe in whose parish it had been found.

Because of this remarkable preservative power, the peat contains a complete and continuous record of its own development which, by methods perfected in this century, can now be read. Plant remains are often preserved in peat in a condition comparable with that of a present day botanical specimen. Of equal or perhaps greater importance is the pollen of trees and other vegetation which grew on and around the accumulating peat and which, wind-blown, was deposited on its surface, became covered, and was preserved. This pollen can be extracted layer by layer, identified in all its different species, and the frequency of each species counted.

A walk across a true peat moor can involve much climbing into and out of the gullies which cut up the peat in many places and which can be many feet deep. In some parts they reach right to the base of the peat where a spread of white sand rests on impervious clay or iron pan. Here you might start reading the story preserved in the peat. Just bring to your memory some of these gullies you have scrambled across, or store this short description to be verified when next you have the chance.

A very few ancient peats contain fragments and pollen of the arctic plants of the nunatakr previously described. They show that some of our moors developed from survivals that weathered the rigours of the last comparatively short glaciation. In that period the ice was almost confined to glaciers in the valleys, to cirques at the valley heads and in the big fells, and to snow-fields on the high ground. The cirques eroded the great bowl-shaped hollows like Combe Scar in Dentdale and Cautley Scar in the Howgills. After the ice had gone there was at first heath moorland with some birch scrub, followed by the return of forests of hazel and pine on the drier parts. On the edges of these forests mesolithic man hunted.

The pine-hazel forest was spreading in a warm climate during the two thousand years of the eighth and seventh millennia BC. There was then a change to wetter conditions in which the pine declined, bogs and peat increased and new woods developed with alder, oak and some elm, for remains and pollen of these are found in the succeeding peat layers. These are woodlands in which Neolithic (New Stone Age) man thrived, and they persisted until about 3000 BC. There followed a dry and warmer spell in which lime and ash trees joined the oak woodland, but the change is marked in all the peats by a very prominent layer of Silver Birch twigs, branches and roots which can scarcely be missed. About 500 B.C. another change of climate to colder and wetter conditions coincided approximately with the invasion of the Celtic Iron Age peoples and the spread of arable and pastoral farming.

Throughout all this succession the woodlands on the uplands were decaying and the spreading bogs and peat were forming our present moorlands. Only a few precious fragments of the early forests now remain to us. One is Colt Park Wood on the east flank of Ingleborough, now a protected and scheduled Nature Reserve. Juniper was one of the early forest invaders, in some parts forming thickets of which we have many traces and two fairly substantial survivors: Moughton on the south-east foot of Ingleborough and, in better condition, on the south side of the Swale opposite Healaugh on the lower slopes of Harkerside. A famous spread of this juniper woodland, just on the fringe of our area, is in Teesdale on the slopes of Mickle Fell near High Force.

W H Pearsall, in his 'Mountains and Moorlands', 1950, summarised all this in one sentence: 'There is, however, little doubt that all the existing upland grassland and much of the moorland, if not all, has been derived from woodland.'

There is a sterner side to the moorlands than the beauty of the autumn heather and the quiet solitude of their wide expanse more appreciated now than in the past. The presence of bogs, frequent and sometimes deep and sometimes extensive, must always have been a standing danger. They often lie close to the tracks and make a moorland crossing hazardous at night or in foggy weather or storm, for in such conditions a track may be easily missed. In clear daylight nature has provided a safeguard and an added beauty, wide spreads of one of the plants that survived the Ice Age and that still thrives in the wetter bogs: this is the Common Cotton Grass *(Eriophorum angustifolium)*. After buttercup and daisy this was the first plant that I was taught to recognise and to beware of. Wandering on the moors with my grandfather, who was devoted to them, or with a great-uncle, a retired Swaledale gamekeeper, I was urgently warned of the significance of this flower by its very practical country name of 'bog-baby-warning', the name by which I yet instinctively think of it.

My companions also taught me of another aspect of the moors in which they both still grudgingly believed but which had been very real indeed to their predecessors. Many superstitions helped to people the moors and dales with other ghostly visitants besides the Whistlers. The most widely known, not only here but over much of Britain and Europe, and by many names, was the dog Barguest. Grandfather referred to him as Guytrash, grandmother as The Soft-footed Hound and occasionally as the Mauthe Dog. By tradition he was a large dog with very big eyes who would appear mysteriously and silently to run beside a traveller for a while, then run off to the side, generally becoming invisible but leaving a visible trail as he disturbed the heather. Sometimes in mischief he would place his paws on his victim's shoulders and would push him over before running away. Some forms of Barguest were more mischievous than others, or more portentous, carrying with them serious warning of trouble.

In certain states of still, hot weather Barguest, as a very small-diameter cyclone, can be seen as a 'windy-willie' making a track across the heather and sometimes, if one is in its path, can even be felt. I was taught to say Greetings to Barguest. There are other 'haunts' of the moors but most of these are tied to a particular place and event and are not, as Barguest was, a universal phenomenon and a normal part of every dalesman's experience and expectation.

The Dales

Mountain peaks and dales are complementary: neither could exist without the other and both are the product of the same erosion. The peaks suffer constant diminution, the dales constant enlargement, but the processes are so slow as to be apprehended only by the geologist. The peaks are still 'the everlasting hills' to which the dale-dweller looks, but the dale is 'home': one's fellows, one's community, one's co-operative institutions secular and religious are located there. The dale dominates the human history of the area but in the physical history it is no less worthy of notice. The whole existence and life of a dale is intimately bound up with its river and its tributaries. Legend often makes the river the goddess of the dale.

The geologist has determined that in general outline, the Dales rivers originated as the drainage pattern of the surface of the uplifted Askrigg Dome, scribed into a cover of rock formations which, by the erosion of rivers and weather, had been completely removed before the last geological period, the Ice Age or Pleistocene. This cover was probably the surface of the chalk, then continuous across the present east Yorkshire, eastwards to some Tertiary sea. As the early rivers deepened their valleys, one, the proto-Humber, having some geological advantage, increased the erosive power of tributaries from both north and south. Thus, during the period that saw the removal of the covering strata from the dome, the tributaries cut off and deflected the Dales rivers, one after another as far north as the Ure.

In the meantime the Swale had been 'captured' by the Tees and it was only during the Ice Age that ice and its deposits deflected the Swale into the Humber-Ouse system. Part of the southern capture were the Don and Dearne via the Trent. Our rivers and dales then, except for minor adjustments of which the Swale represents the largest, were all well-established before the Ice Age. They are very ancient, and by the nature and structure of the rocks through which they run each has attained its own very special character and has won the separate esteem by which each dale is held by its native people to be the best of all.

The largest dale is Wensleydale, more correctly Yoredale, which is notable in that its river, the Ure, has its source in the moss on Lunds Fell where the river Eden also has its origin only a few yards away. The two streams fall into the through-valley of Mallerstang, and turning north and south from Aisgill and White Birch form a river line that links the Irish Sea to the North Sea. Their common valley of Mallerstang has been an important lowland pass through the Pennines throughout historic time, matched only by the more devious and less well-defined passage between the Aire and Ribble, not at their source but in an area near the mid-course of the Ribble.

The many dales, cut to near their present size and shape before the Ice Age, were modified and given many of their present features during that tempestuous and wildly varying period. The Ice Age was indeed not a single event but a period of about a million years marked by vast oscillations of the climate between warm temperate and extreme arctic. At least three arctic glacial episodes were separated by temperate 'interglacials' which were as warm as or even warmer than our present climate. The great ice sheets waxed and waned and, as they were built up by water from the oceans, the quantities locked up in ice were so great as to lower the level of the Earth's seas. During the time of the greatest spread of ice, when it covered the land as far south as the Thames and in many places was several hundreds of feet thick, the sea level was lowered by about three hundred feet. This gave such an added fall to rivers flowing under and from the ice sheets as greatly to strengthen their erosive power. The weight of the ice increased the pressure of the water flowing under it, which thus became a most efficient cutting instrument. We enjoy and admire today some of the results without a thought of the ice continent under which they were created, or a pause to remember the lowered seas which left Britain joined to a continent whose shores were for that time extended to the edge of the Continental Shelf.

There is time to savour all these additional wonders as we walk alone or with a quiet, contemplative friend along the part of the Pennine Way which borders the Kisdon ravine through which the river Swale now flows, leaving its older and boulder-clay-filled valley, Skeb Skeugh, on the other side of Kisdon Hill. This is one of the many gorges in the Dales that were formed under the ice. Some of them are concealed under a cover of the latest boulder-clay deposits; some are still part of the scenery, like the gorge on the Swale at Richmond, and part of the shaping of the valley at the long train of the Aysgarth Falls on the Ure. There is little chance of contemplating the even bigger gorge of the Nidd at Knaresborough except under its temporary cover of pleasure-seeking crowds, but nonetheless we owe it to the same causes.

All the dales have features of similar origin but differing in their scenic detail: Kilnsey Crag and the Netherside gorge in Wharfedale, the gorges on the Clough, many features on the Dee, falls like Hardrow, and scores of the beauty spots for which each dale is famous owe much to the special sculpturing of the Ice Age. The dales have been made U-shaped partly by the ice erosion of the lower slopes of their sides and partly by the flattening of the valley bottom by an infilling of silt. The typical dale is a narrow trough with very steep sides. From Richmond to its head Swaledale never exceeds and is mostly much less than half a mile wide. Half a mile would be an average width for the valley of the Nidd and for Dentdale, Garsdale and Mallerstang, and all the tributary valleys follow the same pattern. Wensleydale is very exceptional in being from the mouth of Mallerstang, a wide valley which because of its width, usually two miles and often three in its lower portion, gives very little impression of its depth. Airedale is somewhat intermediate in its form, but is perhaps more akin to Wensleydale than to the others. A feature, purely the product of the Ice Age, which all the dales share, is the extent of rich and level meadowland in the valley bottom.

The centre of the great ice cap which covered the Dales was over Baugh Fell and Wild Boar Fell, so that the valleys of the Ure and Ribble, which lie more or less radially from this centre, were subject to more intensive erosion and became the two largest dales. The Swale and Nidd did not lie in direct line from the centre and so suffered less intense erosion by the ice but shared in the melt water erosion. The head of Wharfedale, much closed in by the fells, was partly protected.

The melting of the ice cap was not uniform, so that in the colder spells, the snouts of the shrinking glaciers that filled the valleys were almost stationary for a time long enough for the accumulation of debris, which travelled on the surface and also in the body of the ice, to be dropped as terminal moraine across the valley. In the warmer periods the retreat of the ice was comparatively rapid and no moraine was formed. There were seven of these periods of moraine formation and some of the moraines are still prominent features in the valleys. The belt of high gravel across Swaledale at Grinton is one, another is seen across Wharfedale between Grassington and Linton, and many others are conspicuous. They form dry crossing places for the dales roads. Each impounded some of the abundant melt water as a lake, and most of the lakes lasted through prehistoric times and only disappeared as they were concurrently drained by the deepening of the outflow by the enlarged river of melt water, and the infilling by the vast amount of silt carried down. Until well into historic times these lake sites persisted as swamp.

The late glacial period is reckoned to have lasted approximately from 10,000 to 7,000 BC. The silts infilling the lakes and the earliest peats on some of the fells have preserved in great detail the vegetation of the whole period, and at several places gravels and cave deposits contained animal remains. We can therefore confidently complete the picture of our dales at the time when our ancestors were beginning their occupation. The climate and the aspect of the country were those of a frozen tundra like much of Alaska or Siberia today, with the warmer interlude, approximately from 8,800 to 8,000 BC.

A thin scrub of birch and juniper, appearing during the warmer interlude was the forerunner of the returning forests, which gradually spread northwards as the climate returned to temperate after the retreating ice. A description of the fauna may seem to add a touch of fantasy to our picture of the Dales in the later Ice Age. A temperate interglacial had intervened between the glaciation of the south of England and the main Dales glaciation, the end of which we have been discussing. During the early part of this interglacial the abundant melt water swelled the rivers, cut many gorges and deepened the valleys. The climate became mild and the ice disappeared. During that period hippopotamus, rhinoceros and the straight-tusked elephant roamed the dales and their bones have been found in several places in the river gravels and also in caves in Lothersdale near Skipton and at Victoria Cave near Settle. Packs of spotted hyaena preyed on these as well as on other smaller animals and dragged their bones into the caves where they made their dens. In east Yorkshire the Kirkdale Cave had the remains of between two and three hundred hyaena along with gnawed bones of all the other animals.

In another of the warmer interludes it was the giant elk, with its amazing spread of horns, that roamed the moors, which had a rich cover of moorland berries invaded by birch scrub and thickets of juniper. As the cold returned we can picture the landscape much as it is at present, but must people it with reindeer, lynx and bison, with ptarmigan among the birds. The peaks would still have had almost continuous snow cover. The larger mammals were by then extinct, but a new element to be seen would be human hunters. Man's exploitation and appreciation of the landscape had begun and would soon add cultural elements to it.

At this point we can take our leave of the purely physical environment, and a story with its ages to be counted in millions and hundreds of millions of years must give place to the human story whose reckoning will be in centuries and decades. We can now attempt to build up a mental picture of man's arrival in this environment and his eventual conquest of it. Our picture will become steadily fuller as the history becomes more solidly documented. Its centre will always be the people and the evidence of how they lived in the landscape, were influenced by it, and themselves influenced it. Let a flight of ptarmigan or a herd of reindeer crossing the moors be the closing symbol of the protracted ecological story that is the prelude to the life of the Dalesmen, our ancestors.

PART 2: THE PEOPLE
Stone and Bronze

The human history of the Dales begins at the end of the Ice Age, when the glaciers at length disappeared from the cwms at the valley heads leaving only a few snow-covered higher peaks and with a climate still cold and semi-Arctic. On the European Continent beyond the ice sheets various Palaeolithic (Old Stone Age) cultures had been developing, and as the glaciers shrank and the country in the northern parts was gradually cleared of ice a few pioneers followed the edge of the ice, hunting and occupying caves. A few of them came north in Britain as far as some of the caves in Craven, where flint tools have been found dating from the last glacial period, 12,000 to 8,300 BC, the time of our oldest peats, deepest lake silts and of semi-Arctic moorland with scant forest cover.

As the climate became milder and the post-glacial period opened with spreading forests of oak, ash, elm and willow, a new group of humans appeared, moving west from what are now Belgium and France, men who had left the Old Stone Age cultures but were not of the New Stone Age (Neolithic) and so could be called Mesolithic. The English Channel did not yet exist and they could cross a swampy area, now the North Sea, coming in the good seasons year after year but settling in only a very few places such as Star Carr near Scarborough. They are known to the archaeologist as Maglemosian. They were hunters, fishers and food-gatherers, had bows and arrows and spears, made many of their implements of bone or wood and set them with sharp points of flint. Their most distinctive weapon was a harpoon of hard bone, often the shin-bone of a reindeer, or of hard wood, set with tiny barbs of flint. Most of their flint tools, such as knives, and scrapers for dealing with skins, were tiny and these gave rise to the myth of a pigmy people. They were great hunters of the red deer, smaller animals and birds, and were also skilled in trapping some larger animals. At Star Carr and a few other lowland places, they made platforms in the edge of a swamp on which they built permanent settlements of many families, foreshadowing later communities. Occasionally they occupied caves and their tools have been found in several in Craven, with a famous harpoon in Victoria Cave, others in Attermire and a large chisel-like tool of reindeer-horn hafting and wild-boar-tooth blade at Skirethorns Cave. Along the shores of Malham Tarn and the now drained Great Close Tarn, and at many places on the moors at the base of the peat, their tools are abundant.

We do not know how many of these people came, but as they used the moors and dales for a few thousand years it is not surprising that their tiny implements were easily lost and, now refound, are gathered in collections of several thousands in our museums. Usually they are found together with flint chippings and 'cores' of the flint nodules from which they have been chipped, scattered over small but well-defined areas that must have been camping sites used by the same group for year after year and generation after generation.

The climate was steadily improving, becoming warmer and wetter. Thicker forests, with oak, elm, alder and willow in the lower and wetter areas, were spreading and the Pennines were forested up to about 2,000 feet above present sea level. The level of the sea, low during the Ice Age, was rising, and a great river draining south from the swamps that covered much of the present North Sea basin was carving out the early stages of what is now the Channel. During the New Stone Age, starting about 3,000 BC, the severance of Britain from the Continent was completed and newcomers to Britain would have had to use boats.

These newcomers were small pioneer groups. Their origin is not certainly known but probably they were moved, like the Americans who went to colonise the west, partly by increasing population pressure in Europe and partly by an adventurous spirit. In no sense did they set out as martial conquerors. Domestic settlements by these people are very little known, nor have definite field systems been recognised; yet they brought with them the elements of a great revolution in living patterns. It is possible that the Maglemose people saw natural fires started by lightning and conserved and assisted them to make new clearings in the forest in order to extend the grazing areas of deer and other animals that they hunted. The Neolithic folk brought with them the knowledge of fire deliberately made and used as part of their everyday living. They cooked their food and made pottery by its means. They used it along with improved axes to clear places in the forest on which they could grow grain. They were still hunters and still gathered wild fruits, but they were also hunter-farmers who not only sowed seed but had domesticated wild animals, goats, sheep and cattle, used their milk, made cheese from it, and cooked their meat. Dogs had been partly domesticated in Mesolithic times but their complete taming as man's friend and most valuable co-worker was only now achieved. Dogs were probably bred from wolf-cubs brought in by hunters as pets for their children; but grain had been improved from wild stock in the Near East and its use and cultivation was part of the knowledge introduced by the new-comers. As sowing of seed necessitated waiting for the harvest, so Neolithic folk ceased to be wanderers and made permanent homes and settlements.

That the settlers came to all parts of the Dales is abundantly proved not only by their tools but by their pottery, fragments of which are practically imperishable. They are also known by some of their larger monuments, which could only have been built by people living as an organised community. For tools they still used flint but in larger and rougher forms. They made arrow points and a few smaller tools very much in the same style of chipping as the Mesolithic people had used, and may have borrowed this craft from them. They made flint-chipped axes, but added an entirely new resource in the form of fine and smoothly ground stone axes obtained by trade. Their new way of life as farmers was sufficiently productive to provide surpluses that could be used to support other craftsmen. One group found and quarried a fine-grained, very hard and tough volcanic ash on a mountainside in Langdale in the Lake District. From this they roughed out axes and hoes, which were carried over much of the country, even reaching the south, and exchanged for their necessities. The purchasers of the 'roughs' then ground them down to a smooth shape and gave them a good cutting edge. Many have been found in the Dales and every museum has them on exhibit while many are still to be seen in private hands.

With this new tool the settlers made clearances in the forest, supplementing the axe in some places by burning. Tree stumps did not matter as the land between them could be sown, and when the soil fertility was exhausted another patch could be cleared. In all this the settlers were becoming an integrated, independent group for the first time, with leaders and community ritual. One sign of this new style of life is the building of 'henges', of which there are two in the Dales, Castle Dykes at Aysgarth and Yarnbury at Grassington, while the biggest group in the country is at Thornborough Moor only a few miles to the east in the Vale of York. A henge is a large circular platform, sometimes a hundred feet or more in diameter, surrounded by a ditch with a bank outside it. There is always one causeway and sometimes two across the ditch. The henge is certainly a monument of communal significance and use, and it is thought that in any ceremony, religious or civil, the ritual would be performed on the central area by a group of special people while the onlooking 'ordinary' members of the community stood on the surrounding bank, outside the ditch but in good sight and hearing of all that was done. The nature of the ceremony is not known, and it would be presumptuous to name the performers 'priests'. The henges are evidence that their builders were members of a community with more connecting bonds than the trade in axes, and with some degree of philosophy and belief; a thinking, mentally active people that we can look upon as the first real Dalesmen, leaving traces of themselves, domestic and ceremonial, in their tools and structures, and by their exercising an early control of the landscape through forest clearances. Their remains are not very obvious, but all over the Dales we are treading in their footsteps seen and unseen.

About the opening of the third millenium BC there began to come into Britain from the Continent a new people who have been called the Beaker Folk from their pottery, which was associated with their dead, now buried in round barrows. A few of these folk reached westward into the Dales. They mingled peaceably with Neolithic families, borrowed some of their skill as flint-workers to make fine barbed arrow points, and intensified and improved their cattle husbandry. About 2500 BC more of these people began to come to the country in the shape of travelling smiths and tinkers. Some carried small ingots of metal, cut stone moulds, and cast knives and axes at the places they came to for trade. Other folk, related to these but from the Mediterranean area, came by way of Spain to Ireland, where they built many stone circles and started a culture that later spread to the rest of the British Isles by way of the west coast. They were the builders of great stone monuments, Stonehenge and smaller circles and elaborations of the Neolithic 'long barrows' and chambered burials. The stone circles in the Dales are on too small a scale to attract the notice of guide-book writers except for the outstanding Devil's Arrows near Boroughbridge, thought to be the scant remains of a very large circle indeed, and the small but perfect roadside circle at Yockenthwaite. Each dale, however, has at least one or two circles and in some dales a dozen or more are known and it is certain that more, hidden in the heather of the moors, remain to be discovered. These widespread stone circles are the successors of the Neolithic henges, and the Dales people who used and venerated them were also bound together by shared beliefs.

The mingling of late Neolithic and Beaker folk, and then the arrival of bronze pedlars from the east, and of the Megalithic (great stone) builders from Ireland marked the beginning of the Bronze Age. The Bronze Age peoples included a military aristocracy who invaded the south and against whom the Neolithic hill forts were built. From Ireland, trade routes were developed across to the English west coast; one followed the Lancashire Calder up over the moors round Colne, crossed Airedale to pass along Rombalds Moor into lower Wharfedale and so to the great Escrick moraine near York, and on into the east and North Yorkshire Moors. The climate became warmer and drier, and with the new bronze tools forest clearance became possible on an even wider scale. Some tracks across our moors that are still in use today were roughed out by the pedlars and are among the oldest elements in our heritage. Known meeting-places, which might almost be regarded as primitive markets, were established. Many of the lines of our present map were first sketched in during these remote times, and when recognised deserve respect. The Bronze Age people had grown wheat but their great contribution to the agriculture of the Dales, apart from their greater interest in, and skill with cattle, was the cultivation of barley. They used much more personal ornament, and necklaces of jet, many of them from the Whitby coast, were buried in their round barrows. Among the 'rulers' gold ornaments from Ireland were widely used. Finer pottery was made, at first for vessels associated with the new burial customs that were possibly dictated by new beliefs, but gradually for domestic uses also. Weaving of cloth was greatly improved. All this makes up a picture of communities of a simple farming peasantry continuing and improving the Neolithic pattern of life while accepting a small aristocracy of Bronze Age incomers who added much to their culture and crafts. Gradually the 'native' descendants of Mesolithic and Neolithic folk peacefully combined with and absorbed the various Bronze Age incomers, and this new and virile population expanded rapidly, spreading right across the Pennines.

The Coming of the Celts

A further change in the climate in about 500 BC to conditions colder and wetter than at present, together with a rapid increase in the population, may have been responsible for a western migration from Central Europe by which Iron Age people, the Celts, arrived in Britain during the sixth and fifth centuries BC. These Hallstadt, Austrian people were prosperous farmers, and miners of iron and salt; but they were aggressive and military minded, with chiefs to lead them and with armour and weapons of iron superior to anything the Bronze Age had. They attacked and conquered much of the south and south-east of England, but had little contact with the north except for a settlement at Scarborough Castle Hill. In the third century BC a second group of Iron Age people, the La Tene, followed and, entering Yorkshire by the Humber estuary and passing up the various rivers, penetrated all the dales. On the Pennines the Celts joined the confederacy of the Brigantes, a powerful tribal group ruled by a king and with a capital at Castle Hill, Almondbury near Huddersfield. They had a measure of 'civilisation': while inheriting and continuing many of the crafts of the Bronze Age, the Celts also brought with them, in their migration from the Continent, skills in metal-working and enamelling that they had acquired by contact with the Mediterranean peoples. They used a gold coinage, made splendid enamelled brooches, mirrors and shields and had a wide range of iron tools. They were great breeders of horses. The Dales are in every part enriched by their visible remains, to be numbered at least in several hundreds. There are many places where Celtic fields and huts, cattle pounds, burial mounds and roads, with all the adjuncts of a large community, are to be seen in their entirety on common pasture ground. This has never been ploughed or disturbed, except by grazing sheep, since the fields were newly turned over by the simple breast-plough of a Celtic peasant. The two or three hundred acre site at Lea Green, Grassington, or the almost equal sites at Carpley Green and round the flanks of Addlebrough in Wensleydale are only the more easily accessible examples.

This Celtic way of life flourished until challenged by Roman invasions. By the middle years of the first century AD the challenge reached the country of the Brigantes with war nearing them on the Welsh borders. Caractacus, who had led the resistance to the Romans in Wales and been defeated, sought refuge with his relation, Cartimandua, who was queen of the Brigantes; but she, pro-Roman, sold him as a prisoner to the enemy and put herself under their protection in the town that they had established at Aldborough (Isaurium) near Boroughbridge. Her husband Venutius, a native Brigantian and our first named folk-hero, raised the Brigantes to oppose the Romans. The great camp on the summit of Ingleborough, where the foundations of a large number of his huts are still plain to be seen and to excite the knowledgeable observer, was made his capital and many great earthworks, among them the Ta Dyke across the Stake Pass, the look-out fortlet at Gregory, Grassington, and the complex of the Fremington Dykes in Swaledale were constructed, along with the early defences at Stanwick Park just north of Richmond.

In spite of all this war preparation the Dalesfolk continued in their Celtic way of life, only answering Venutius' call to work on, and later to defend, these many points of resistance as the Roman attack became more immediately threatening. The Roman general Agricola tried to isolate the people of the Dales with his framework of roads and with police camps like that of Bainbridge at the centre. Life was not entirely peaceful. Some of the many caves excavated in the Dales have queer stories to tell. Several have yielded up smaller objects of obvious plunder from Roman individuals and even from Roman camps. It would not be an improbable picture to imagine a Roman messenger or even an official inadequately escorted, using one of the unguarded roads or a Celtic path, being seized by Celtic brigands and stripped of his plate armour (a valuable source of iron), his shield, knife, and anything else that might be of use immediately or as raw material. The scene of the Roman soldier returning saddened and disgraced to camp with a terrible tale of his encounter with the wild Brigantes, cannot have been an uncommon one. The Bainbridge police camp was more than once burnt down and rebuilt following the attentions of the 'natives'. In the Dales then, the Celts remained an intransigent folk taking little of the Roman culture and keeping much to their own way of life. A few of the Roman skills and fashions, such as the occasional rectangular hut, or the inclusion of a few families in the civilian settlements round the military camps produced a Romano-British culture, but at the withdrawal of the Roman troops at the beginning of the fifth century it was a Celtic-style peasantry that remained in the Dales. This gradually declined; younger families moved into the Vale of York to enjoy the easier conditions of the richer land, or into the valley bottoms where extensive settlements grew up, with dwellings clustered in one part of an area of fields and cattle-pounds and surrounded by a heavy defensive bank. Such defended settlements can be seen at Outgang near Kilnsey and at Thornber near Arncliffe; similar settlements, but without the defensive bank, are at Stridebuts near Malham, Southerscales on Ingleborough side, Carpley Green near Bainbridge and other places in the Dales. Some are surviving Bronze Age and Celtic settlements, but a few are indubitably later Celtic-Romano-British sites. Near the huts there are many small irregular cultivation patches and larger stock-pounds, but the rest of the site is usually a series of long, narrow and parallel fields, almost prototypes of the Anglian lyncheted fields. They must have been ploughed by ox-drawn ploughs — or perhaps horses were used. These ploughed fields were probably copied from those of the Roman villa farms. The possibility is becoming increasingly recognised that such prosperous settlements on the flatter lands near the rivers may have been the lure that induced the next wave of migrants to attack and take them over. Otherwise the Anglian penetration of the Dales seems to have been a fairly peaceful occupation of valley lands not taken up by the 'hill-man' Celts.

Angles, Danes, Norsemen

The newcomers were the Angles, probably from Frisia in northern Germany (Lower Saxony) and southern Denmark. A part of the Celtic population had formed a small confederation within the forest of Elmet, which extended between the lower valleys of the rivers Wharfe, Aire and Calder. The opposition of Elmet was strong enough to hinder penetration of these dales on any large scale until conquered by the Anglian King Edwin soon after 616. With this Anglian presence the Dales began to take on their modern character, many new villages being founded in the seventh century with characteristic plans that can still be recognised in their modern configuration.

The Angles were in many ways a sharp contrast to the Celts whom they were to neighbour and who would eventually absorb them. The short and sturdy Celts had chosen to live on the more open higher lands of the Dales, hunting in the forests, making only small clearings for grazing their cattle and pigs and practising agriculture only on a smallholding or allotment scale. They were, however, breeders and venerators of the horse, an animal scarcely used at all by the Angles. The tall and fair Angles were powerfully built, blue-eyed with fair or red hair, skilled in arable farming and in forest clearing. Their strength was used in reclaiming enough land for fields of ploughland. They depended on the powerful, stolid ox for most of their work. This use of oxen continued into the Middle Ages and the ox's capacity in daily work became the basis of our measures of length and area, such as furlong and acre, only now being abandoned, to the regret and puzzlement of some of us, in favour of the foreign metric measures.

The houses of the new villages were arranged around a central space still often recognizable as the village green. They were small, built of timber and thatched, and accompanied by barns and other farm outbuildings making a rectangular group. Behind the houses, each built on a toft, were the small crofts within an encircling fence. Animals could be herded into the central space for safety from wolves and other predators, and on occasion from marauding neighbours, 'landless men' who included 'outlaws', or, a more serious threat, the raids of Picts and Scots. The earliest of these settlements, possibly of the sixth century, had names in the form of Cowling or Addingham, the *ing* portion meaning 'the people of ...', but these are rare. The main invasion reached into the Dales via the river valleys in the late sixth and seventh centuries. The invaders chose good bottom lands, river terraces and patches of glacial gravel for their villages of traditional form, but only where they could clear sufficient land from the surrounding forest for their ploughland. This was the immediate task in order to secure a source of regular food. On the higher land they had to find or make pasture for cattle, and places where they could safely graze their pigs. Cleared timber was used for houses and fences. It is hard to visualise the tremendous sense of urgency that must have stimulated the strenuous activity of a small but tightly knit community making a home in a strange and threatening environment.

In their homeland they had been organised into groups of usually nine or ten families, and in their new land they kept to this pattern. Each group forming a village needed about the same amount of land, and so the villages were spaced at roughly three mile intervals along the valleys and varied only in response to the shape of the valley with an occasional gorge. The clearing originally required for the ploughlands and pastures, recorded in the eleventh-century Domesday survey, had been a gigantic task for generation after generation of men who had worked to exhaustion. It would be impossible to overestimate their grit and determination if some reflection of it were not still to be seen in the present stubborn persistence that is a part of the true Dalesman's character. Dalesmen of not very distant generations have completed comparable tasks in creating the hundreds of miles of dry stone walling along the valleys and over the wildest fells, or in driving scores or even hundreds of miles of levels through resistant rocks within the vast network of the now abandoned mines.

The villages settled between the sixth and eleventh centuries follow a regular pattern that can to a large extent be traced in their naming. The suffix 'leah', now modified to 'ley', was given to a village made in a forest clearing. The long chain of villages, now towns, in Airedale between Leeds and Skipton have almost all names ending in 'ley' from Armley to Bradley, and this tells us something of the extent of forest. Skipton, at the beginning of the more open country of the limestone, is only one of the now common names ending in 'ton'. These are later than the 'leys' and signify single farms enclosed from the waste by later arrivals, or by sons of a later generation moving out from settled villages as population increased.

It would be difficult to overestimate what we owe to these Anglian farmer-settlers. Our small parish councils of today are a remnant shadow of the Anglian village gathering that managed all the affairs of the *township*. Townships were gathered into larger groups, the *wapentakes*, containing originally ten townships but later more as population and number of townships increased. Wapentakes are still with us as the areas by which magistrates' courts and many police operations, such as licensing, are defined. Only within the last few decades have the Anglian divisions of counties and ridings been disrupted, rearranged and often renamed, to our sorrow and confusion with little advantage gained.

Each village was a close-knit unit with many family relationships, and with a leading headman, one of themselves. He had a somewhat larger house, which in later centuries under the feudal system often became the 'hall' or manor house. When remnant Celts were taken into these communities they were in some degree an acceptable acquisition. The Angles worshipped a variety of nature gods. The Celts also had many nature gods: in particular they venerated trees, and among their crafts had a great knowledge of the forests among which the new settlements were being made. Celts were most valued and perhaps feared for the magical powers attributed to the worker in iron, as well as for their skill with horses. The new villages needed for their buildings, their tools and their ploughs, the woodman and blacksmith: both of these could be supplied by the Celts. It may be from this that forester and blacksmith held, all through the Middle Ages, something of a special position in the villages. For the Celts the horse held a big place in their mythology, with the smith as its servant and master. The smith therefore, whether Celt or Angle, was always even to recent times an important man, often the 'wise man' of the village, the symbol of rural life adopted by poet and story-teller, and his smithy was always the focal point, the bright gleaming eye of the village. The Village Blacksmith under the spreading tree still moves the hearts and imaginations of the older generation even now. Another thing that we probably owe to the Celts is the Dalesman's traditional love of horses. 'Shake a bridle over a Dalesman's grave and he will get up' was a saying truer a couple of generations ago than now, but none the less indicative of a deep-ingrained love of horses. Gypsies and especially tinkers have much affinity with the Celts and still, like many good Dalesmen, they congregate at the horse-fairs where they are entirely at home and a part of the goings-on and not just visitors like the curious 'offcomer'.

The Celts and Angles were pagans but Edwin, king of Northumbria, was baptised at York in 617 by Paulinus, a missionary from Rome who preached to the Angles, built a church at York and baptised large crowds in the Swale near Catterick. Within six years Penda of Mercia invaded Deira (the southern part of Northumbria) and returned the Angles to their paganism, but this was only a brief interlude. Monks, brought by Aidan from the Irish Celtic Church of Iona, settled their monastery at Lindisfarne in 634 and going out from there as missionaries brought the Angles back to Christianity, but to the practices of the Celtic not the Roman church; and so Celtic influence was again strong on the Pennines, and remained so even though the Synod of Whitby in 663 reintroduced the Roman form. From the eighth to the eleventh century the wooden preaching rod or 'staff-rood' was set up at many places where people could gather from more than one village. At some of these a small timber church was built and ground set aside as a burial place. Many of these are the churches named in the Domesday survey and they became the parish churches. Bishop Wilfrid, from his minster at Ripon, had great influence in the Dales and many parish churches were built. A priest cared for the population of many townships which then made up, and to a large extent still make up, the very extensive parishes characteristic of the region.

When churches with graveyards were established, the custom of setting up a stone shaft (a Celtic custom) or a cross spread from the monasteries of Hexham and Ripon. The earliest crosses are in the eastern part of the Dales; those at Ilkley and Otley were erected probably before or about 800 AD. Their ornament shows much Celtic influence in the interlacing patterns and vine scroll decoration and in some of the animal motifs that cover them. The same influence is also seen on many of the later crosses that came from a school of carvers at Ripon and spread to many churches in the lower dales.

At the end of the eighth century and during part of the ninth, the raids of Danish pirates on the coast destroyed the peace of the north. Half a century of war and rapine followed in all the eastern part of England and by 867 York was captured. In that year Halfdan the Dane conquered Northumbria and made a peace that allowed his army to seek settlement all over the conquered areas. The Danes settled mostly on the rich lands of the Vale of York and in the lower dales. Their settlements may often be recognised by names ending in *thorpe,* though this may have come in a little later. They seem to have made their settlements on land that was unoccupied, filling in between the Anglian villages; and the termination *thorpe* appears in most cases to signify a dependent farm or hamlet linked with an Anglian township, for example Burnsall-with-Thorpe. The name 'kirkby' denoted a village with a church, and occurs in two forms, one of location and one personal: Kirkby Lonsdale and Kirkby Stephen. All this suggests a peaceful penetration so that many of the Dales villages must have been equally familiar with a few persons of dark and wiry appearance and Celtic descent, and the strikingly tall and fair Danes who in many ways matched the Angles. By intermarriage the newcomers were gradually absorbed into the dominant Anglian population.

The early years of the tenth century saw the last and very significant addition to the complex folk character that we are recognising as the traditional Dalesman. In the sixth and seventh centuries various domestic pressures and the spirit of adventure had taken the Norse seamen, the Vikings, from the western parts of Norway to Orkney and Shetland. After making further major settlements in uninhabited Iceland, they moved round the Scottish Coasts and Western Isles eventually to reach and colonise Northern Ireland, creating their town of Dublin. The linguistic evidence supports the idea that in the Scottish islands and in Ireland they mingled peaceably with the native Celts. During the tenth century further movement took them to the Isle of Man, where again they joined in peace with the Celtic population. From this base they spread into the Wirral and, in large numbers, into the south Lakeland fells and valleys. Some of them, still seeking fell and dale country, made the easy expansion onto the sparsely occupied land around the Ribblehead nexus of fells, of Dentdale, Garsdale and the heads of Widdale, Wharfedale and Airedale. Mallerstang was an open road to the upper valley of the Ure and to the fells at the head of the Swale.

The Norsemen, mingling and intermarrying with the Celts, soon developed a Norse-Irish strain in their language and names. They were great sheep farmers and the uplands of the Pennines were very suitable land on which to locate their farms. It was as well that this was the least desirable land for the Anglian arable farmers. The Norse farms were generally well spaced out in order that each might have its own sheep-run without danger of the flock mixing with those of the neighbours. This system was the opposite of the close-knit Anglian village community; yet despite such sturdy, assertive independence immediate and unlimited assistance was always available from the nearest neighbour in any emergency. These characteristics were transmitted to those who inherited the Norsemen's genes, so that this almost aggressive self-sufficiency is still a hallmark of the true-born Dalesman. Amity with the Anglo-Danes, with whom the Norsemen lived side by side, was possible because the incomers made no demand on the same land, but sought and were contented with what to the already settled villagers was 'the waste'.

As sheep farmers, the Norse-Irish required two sets of pasture, in summer on the fells and in winter in the higher valleys. We can picture a Norse settler named Gunnar, typical of many, who with others — among whom may have been Shunner and Rafn — found his way by Mallerstang into Swaledale. Choosing unoccupied pasture near the foot of a gill and a position on a limestone terrace he built his house of timber on a substantial stone foundation. This would be not very unlike the houses of the Anglian villages though larger and possibly more solid. It was his *saetr,* the house for his summer grazing on the fells above and his shelter for winter when he kept his flock on the pastures around and below him. Gunnar, a tall, fair, silent shepherd, would be seen striding about the fells and coming occasionally into the villages down dale to barter wool for corn and other goods. Descendants and friends moved onto the dry gravel-spread of the large beck that flowed in Gunnar's gill, used the riverside meadows and made their hamlet there. This was accepted by the local population and in time called Gunnar's saetr; by 1633 it had become Gunnersett and now Gunnerside. Another early Norse settlement is Thwaite, 'a clearing of meadow or pasture', near the head of the valley. Other place-names of this form are spread over the valley heads, Burtersett, Countersett, Ravenseat, Appersett and many others, each in time the nucleus of a later hamlet.

The foundations of what may indeed have been Gunnar's house at Winterings are those of a typical 'long house'. Of these Norse or early medieval houses over forty have been found, mostly at about the 1,000 feet level on the rough limestone pasture. With the help of a small group of students I have surveyed them, and the survey shows that these 'long houses' are usually solitary, only very rarely in a group of three or four together. They are spread all over the limestone dales, now just foundations about 30 feet long and from 12 to 15 feet wide. Usually there is a partition across the centre dividing the house into two rooms. In one of them is a fireplace, sometimes in the middle, sometimes in one corner or against a wall; this was of course the living-room. The other, outer room was used on occasion to shelter cattle. The entrance to the house was sometimes in this compartment or else near the end of the partition. Contemporary with the 'saetrs' and equally Norse were the 'scales' (from the Norse *skali*), temporary huts often associated with cattle, and these, though not so numerous as the 'setts', are found all over the western part of the Dales — Winterscales, Barden Scale, Souther-scales are just some of many — and they mark places where the Norsemen practised some degree of cattle-breeding.

The Vikings, as well as being great adventurers by sea, were great traders by both sea and land. By 919 they had captured York, established as a trading centre by the Romans, and maintained as such by the Angles and Danes. After the capture of the city the Vikings quickly expanded its function as a fortified market town with an almost cosmopolitan population that may have numbered near ten thousand souls. Shops, craftsmen's workshops, moneyers' mints and all the mercantile adjuncts of the second largest city in the country were soon developed. A joint kingdom between York and Dublin was set up and lasted, with only a short intermission, until 954. The traffic of traders, messengers, officials and many other folk backwards and forwards between the two cities had to be conducted by way of Pennine crossings, and so for several decades the villages along the route must have been kept lively by the passage of a great variety of people from the outside world. There must have been some 'staging' or resting places on these routes, and no doubt some villages profited by this. One of them may have been Yockenthwaite in Langstrothdale, for its name 'Yoghan's thwaite' is suggestive. 'Yoghan' is the Norse adaptation of a native Celtic name Eogan, and 'thwaite' is a forest clearing. A survey of the area has revealed a group of Norse-style 'long houses', their foundations still plain on the common around the present farms of Yockenthwaite, and many Norse-Irish names occur in the neighbourhood. This familiarity with traders and trade in part prepared the Dales for the introduction of local markets near the forests, which later supplemented the few regional markets of the Normans.

The apparent peace of the eleventh century was broken by renewed Danish raids and in 1016 Cnut, son of the king of Denmark, defeated the English Edmund and became king of England. He created four Earldoms, one being Northumbria. The greatest change for the Pennines was the king's declaration of some of the more thinly populated areas as royal forests, reserved for his hunting and subject to new forest laws. The royal forests continued for a few centuries to be areas within which the preservation of deer and other game took precedence over all else, and the small population allowed to remain within them was reduced to a strict serfdom under a bureaucracy of forest officials. Cnut's great forest of the north included some of the north-western parts of the Dales including Dentdale and Garsdale. In the south-east was the forest of Knaresborough.

Norman Conquest

When the Normans conquered England in 1066, they adopted these forests and continued them under even stricter laws; they also created many smaller ones under the governance of some of their chief tenants. These were subject to all the forest laws but had the status of a 'chase'. Several were created in the Dales: Litton Forest, Langstrothdale Chase, Wensleydale Forest, Bowland Forest, Swaledale Forest, New

Forest, Arkengarthdale Forest and others. Most of these persisted until the fifteenth or sixteenth century with little modification.

By the mid-eleventh century England was united and Angle, Dane, Norse and remnant Celt had become roughly integrated, at least sufficiently to make an English people. The military rule and feudal organisation at once imposed on them by Norman William made great changes in their life, from some of which we still suffer. The land that had belonged to the peasant communities was declared to be the possession of the king, and the native peasantry became serfs, a euphuism for slaves. The land with its townships was distributed in generous grants among William's relatives and supporters, all like himself 'offcomers' (as the Dalesman would call them) or foreigners. Little of these grants has come back to the people, and when land that had remained crown property was sold off in the seventeenth century, it was to private buyers. The Dales were among the earliest areas in our part of the north to be shared out among the Normans. Alan Rufus, cousin of William, was given 242 townships in Yorkshire; most of them were in the North Riding and formed the Honour of Richmond. Comparable 'Honours' were formed at Skipton and Middleham, and with these the disposal of the Dales was almost complete.

Within three years of the conquest a rebellion was understandably threatened in the north, and William responded with a murderous expedition bringing massacre, burning and almost total devastation to the centre of Yorkshire and much of Durham. Alan Rufus accompanied and assisted him in this 'Harrying of the North'. To prevent further troubles, and also to ward off attack from Scotland, castles were built as centres of military strength. They also served for the control of the local populations, which had little kindly feeling towards their conquerors. The Anglo-Danes had adopted Gilling and Catterick as the chief places of their administration, but Alan ignored these and chose an almost isolated rocky headland in a bend of the River Swale on the edge of the forest of Marwood, which he fortified and made the site of his castle, giving it the new name of Richmond. Starting in 1071 and employing masons from Normandy with abundant local serf labour, he replaced his first wooden castle by the splendid stone structure, the remains of which are still there, the admiration of thousands of today's tourists. This work took twenty years. Between 1170 and 1174 Alan's great-nephew Conan added the magnificent keep. In and around the castle Alan housed his small army of military followers and rewarded many of them with manors and estates, as tenants of which they rendered military and castle service in lieu of rent. Their duties included keeping the Dalesfolk in order and subjection. Castles were also built at Skipton and Middleham.

Within Richmond Castle there were many officials and a host of servants. The lord's immediate household was properly housed in Scolland's Hall and the garrison in military quarters, but the mass of servants slept wherever they could find room to lie down. The chief officials of the castle and Honour were the Steward, Constable and Chamberlain; minor officials were Butlers, Sheriffs and Lardiners, the last being the various officers responsible for collecting and disposing of food supplies. The army of military followers and the whole castle population were fed and maintained by compulsory levies on the crops and stock of the many villages of the Honour. The Domesday survey of 1098, which was to record the taxable value of the country, lists most of the lowland villages of the Vale of York as completely devastated and waste, but this was not the condition in the Dales. Some villages were held by king's thanes — Angles who had accepted the Norman rule. The Domesday survey, however, did not extend north of the Tees nor westward as far as the head of the Dales rivers. Reeth was the last village listed in Swaledale, Askrigg (Fors) in Wensleydale, Hubberholme in Wharfedale and Settle in Ribblesdale. This Pennine 'edge' to the Domesday survey can be seen from the other side to be the outer edge of the great pre-conquest forests confirmed by William and exempt from the taxation. These forests were largely coterminous, for Swaledale, Wensleydale, Langstrothdale and Litton, Mewith with the Celtic town of Dent at its centre, all had common boundaries one with another.

In none of these forest areas were there villages, but Celts had lived in them and the Norse had made their many small clearings for setts and scales. These were accepted by the Normans but converted into 'vaccaries'. These were small fenced areas of cleared land with one or two small crofts and a keeper's hut. His duty was to cherish the deer and to give his cattle carefully controlled grazing in the forest. He might also keep pigs, grazing them on the abundant mast. The forest-dwelling Norseman had to give up many of his sheep, for their grazing on the tree saplings was eventually the greatest factor in deforestation. He could, however, still keep some sheep on the treeless fells.

Each forest had its Warden, a wealthy and powerful baron or feudal tenant, or tenant-in-chief who, like Alan, held his land directly from the king. Under his control were several foresters and the Woodmote and Swainmote Courts to administer the forest law, which was very severe and differed in many articles from the common law. 'Verderers' and 'Woodwards' were officers of the courts charged with the care and oversight of trees, timber and game. The foresters had many duties including the control of wolves, trespassers and poachers, the repair of hedges and, as with all other officers, the protection and care of the deer. To accommodate his foresters the Warden was required to build houses for them in a new village, where they would not become too good neighbours with potential trespassers and poachers. In 1227 one Ranulph, in reply to a *quo warranto*, testified that his ancestors had raised the town of Bainbridge, with houses for twelve foresters, each house with nine acres of ground, in the Earl's forest of Wensleydale. The foresters took oath not to wrong beasts or trees. Occasionally a forester was privileged to enclose and clear a little extra land to improve his small-holding, but deer had to be unmolested if they came over his fence, which had to be restricted in height. Similar villages for foresters are Healaugh for the forests of Swaledale, Arkengarthdale and the New Forest; Buckden for Litton and Langstroth Forests; Horton for the forest of Mewith, and others outside the Dales.

The foresters and officers, with the Norse settlers in setts and scales, together made up a small population, and to supply the basic needs of those who did not leave the forest or travel far, small customary markets, without any charter, grew up on the borders of the forest and near the foresters' villages. Kettlewell, Askrigg and Grinton (later Reeth) were all forest markets to which came pedlars and local farmers rather than merchants. Here news and gossip would be gathered and some contact made between forest and Dalesfolk, but otherwise the forests were a secluded and private world. They were not by any means all unbroken woodland, but comprised not only thickly wooded lowland but also much bare fell country and moorland, yet all the land was reserved for hunting. These uplands and some of the woodland were the territories that had been occupied by Celtic and Norse settlers and so remained the natural reserve of Celtic and Scandinavian lore, legend and beliefs, and the areas where the 'old religion' longest survived the attack of Christianising missions. They were the home ground of witchcraft and spells, wise men and wise women, omens and signs.

One example of Celtic myth, the drowned village of Semer Water, is almost tiresomely over-quoted, and yet it deserves respect for its age and ancestry. Semer Water, a glacial lake survival, lies in a hollow, rich in historic and prehistoric associations. At the two ends of the lake are the Norse settlements of Marsett and Countersett, at its head the deep forested dales of Raydale and Bardale once inhabited by wolves and suitable ground for a wealth of grisly legend and story. On the east side of the lake are the extensive Celtic Iron Age settlements of Carpley Green with the earlier monument of High Raise, a Bronze Age burial mound. During the very low water levels of the drought in 1923, the dwelling platform of a Bronze Age family, with archaeological remains demonstrating a very long occupation, were uncovered and explored. The original drowning of this by a rise of the lake level took place somewhere about the Iron Age, and a folk memory of the event could not escape engaging the imagination of both Celtic and Norse story-tellers. In the medieval period it was inevitable that zealous churchmen should Christianise the legend and that much later the Victorian romantics welcomed and elaborated it in prose and verse. Only Granville Bantock in recent times has restored its dignity and proper status in a splendid musical setting.

As wolves were the terror of the early forests, they naturally took foremost place in the legends of the Dales as in those of the Black Forest. Fear of wolves probably lies behind such stories as those of the Penhill giant's dog Wolfhead and of Barguest.

The forests were also, throughout the Middle Ages, a refuge for outlaws, and indeed the forest laws helped to create this class. Outlaws from time to time preyed on the travellers, and so arose a whole corpus of 'Robin Hood stories', some of which had sufficient substance and appeal to become popular ballads and tales. During this period, however, the fashion for hunting, for which the forests had originally been designated, declined, and they progressively disintegrated under the pressure for 'assarts', that is clearances and enclosures for agriculture.

A most important element that has influenced all the life of the Dalesfolk is the existence of markets and traders. The Norman castles with their army of followers created an immediate problem in the supply of food, both in respect to quantity and quality. Apart from the lord's demands, his garrison and his supporters included a large proportion of foreigners who wanted much more than the meagre and restricted diet that could be levied from the Dales population. Wines and the more exotic foods, silks and fine cloths, armour and a great many other goods were demanded and had to be imported by merchants who could only bring them in under the protection of the castle and its garrison. Markets almost international in character were soon established at the chief castle towns. To them the nearer Dalesfolk came for such necessities as they could not themselves produce, probably obtaining them by barter of their few surpluses, wool, skins, lead and perhaps cheese. Some Dalesmen bred hunting dogs, much favoured by the Normans.

The social importance of the markets must have been very great. A section of the Dalesfolk saw and perhaps met and bargained with merchants from towns and occasionally even from foreign countries. On a smaller scale we have seen that a few forest markets had been formed by the beginning of the thirteenth century. Their convenience was appreciated, and they were followed by the establishment of small local markets in the larger villages. These had two effects upon the Dalesman's life, effects that in some measure persisted almost to the present century. The standard of life of the increasing number of small yeoman farmers was improved and they could employ labourers. To some extent also, these early markets were responsible for a liberation of the Dalesfolk from the cramping servitude to the feudal landlords that had been imposed on them under the Norman conquest. Most of the peasants had become serfs compelled to work at least half their time on the lord's demesne. The Black Death of the fourteenth century so reduced their numbers that it became almost impossible to keep the land in cultivation even with the most rigorous legal enforcements. In these circumstances wage labour and the commutation of feudal services into money rent became common. A few serfs were able to take advantage of these conditions to increase their own small landholdings, to trade their surpluses in the markets and through buying their freedom, to move from the class of serf into the new status of small-holder or yeoman and themselves become employers of labour. Secondly the yeoman-farmer had to find a market for his produce. He therefore travelled a little to find the best outlet and so met farmers from a wider area. Through business links and friendships thus established, through the meeting of women at market with their cheese, butter and other small produce, and through daughters going into service with people met at market, marriages took place between families more widely separated than hitherto. The social horizon was expanded from the village to the market area and soon the wider circle of neighbouring dales. By this process my own family has drawn members from the dales of Swale, Ure, Aire and Calder in the last four generations, and by collaterals from the rest of the dales.

For the growth and success of markets in the countryside, the first necessity was free movement between them. The passage of soldiers and officials between the castles had created a sparse network of military roads patterned upon and partly using the Roman ones. Ancient tracks between villages and new market centres, not only down the length of a dale but across the intervening moors, were more regularly trodden and became indelibly engraved on the landscape. The users of this growing network of tracks (only in comparatively recent times did some of them take on the semblance of roads) were many and various but remained the same for many centuries. Mounted on horseback and wearing expensive cloaks to protect fine clothes and keep out the cold, the merchants would be accompanied by their purser to look after money matters, a scribe to keep their accounts, sometimes a priest to keep them safe from the Devil and his minions. They would be followed by their personal servants and horse keepers, goods on pack ponies, two or three or even a full train of twenty, and above all a bodyguard of bowmen and swordsmen to deal with Robin-Hood-type adventurers. Two or three merchants and an occasional money-changer would make up a very imposing cavalcade, a spectacle and a gossip-worthy event to be reported by marketing peasants to smaller villages and remote hamlets. Many would attempt, for their own safety, to travel in the shadow of the cavalcade.

There too, would be the humbler huckster with his single 'galloway' or 'gell' bearing the elementary means of displaying his bundle of goods, pedlars and chapmen who dealt in pence where merchants dealt in nobles. Minstrels, conjurors, entertainers of many kinds might mix with the procession and collect a few pence for lightening the tedium of the journey or amusing the sober crowd at the next market.

The Monasteries

In the twelfth and thirteenth centuries the Dales were subjected to a second set of foreign overlords, this time not military but ecclesiastical, through the introduction of monastic communities. These, originating from Continental monasteries and owing close allegiance to them, were nevertheless of far greater benefit to the native Dalesfolk than were the feudal barons who, though they might offer some small measure of protection against outside enemies, were still in the main exploiters. For the salvation of their guilty souls and as prepayment for heavenly well-being, the lords not only offered assistance to the Crusades but also gave large areas of their wilder lands to the monasteries, whose original object was, like that of the numerous hermits, to promote an ascetic life of prayer and pious meditation in a wilderness removed from the temptations of the world.

Such was the ideal but, alas, too many things were against its continuance. The temptations from which the monks had fled followed to the gates of the monasteries, their estates were enriched and in time trade, agriculture, sheep farming and elaborate building employed growing numbers of servants and tenants. As their buildings grew, 'for the glory of God', to the magnificence that we now appreciate in their ruins, so debts grew commensurately; spirituality and the ascetic life declined until the end came with the sixteenth century Reformation. This four-century episode was, however, powerful in influencing the life-style of a large proportion of Dalesfolk.

The founders of the monasteries came from areas of France such as Brittany where agriculture flourished, and according to the resources of the district, special skills were practised. The White Monks of the Cistercian order, the first to settle within the Dales, came from the district of Citeaux where the natives had a well-developed arable agriculture and were also breeders of sheep and dealers in wool on a large scale. In addition they were skilled smelters and workers in iron. The large grants of land in the dales, fells and valleys were ideal country for sheep runs, and the lowlands off the Pennines provided areas for extensive arable farms while some of the Millstone Grit country supplied the more easily smelted iron ores that could sustain a moderate iron industry.

The secular estates of the monasteries were managed from 'granges', each the head of a district estate extending for a few miles around it. Kilnsey, one of the many granges belonging to Fountains Abbey, ruled most of the land between the rivers Wharfe and Ribble above Threshfield and Horton to the river heads. The grange was connected to the parent abbey by a road, which in time was made wide enough for the passage of wagons. Bridges were built where needed for the crossing of difficult streams, the one at Appletreewick over the River Dibb and one at Conistone being by later tradition credited to the Devil. This road after reaching Kilnsey continues as Mastiles Lane over the moors to the Malham estates and then north to the Fountains estates in Borrowdale. Along all the length of the road, and others like it, the monks secured the right to pass with their sheep and cattle and to lodge them overnight at many places along the journey.

The officers of the monastery made regular visits to the granges. The Cellarer came at short intervals to examine accounts and to hold courts. Frequently he was accompanied by the Prior and even on occasion by the Abbot. Always the officials travelled in state, with a large body of servants and sufficient bodyguards, in a considerable and colourful procession. Dalesfolk all along the route would come from remote dwellings to see this pageant and get a blessing from one or other of the holy travellers. This was by no means a free treat as the train had to be fed by large levies of food from the abbey tenants and this was often a heavy strain on their resources. Dues and rents were collected, farms inspected by minor officials and work checked and set. Mass was performed at the grange and most people from the estate would make effort to attend. So for many generations the monasteries brought into the peasants' hard labouring life an occasional day of pageantry and official blessing or rebuke.

Because the greater part of our remoter dales were of little value except for sheep runs and hunting, it was those that had been given to the monasteries, some of which were far distant. Furness Abbey had large estates at Ribblehead, Ingleborough and in the Winterburn Valley; much of upper Nidderdale belonged to Byland Abbey; Sawley Abbey had Stainforth and much of middle Ribblesdale, and upper Swaledale was held by Bridlington Priory. Of the monasteries sited in the Dales themselves, Jervaulx had most of upper Wensleydale above Askrigg, and so originated the name Abbotside. Bolton Priory had the part of Malham Moor now called Priors Rake in part, with half of Malham and much land around Skipton and in Airedale. The smaller priories of Coverham, Easby and Egglestone belonged to a slightly later order, the Premonstratensian from Premontre; Coverham had estates at Kettlewell in Wharfedale and had with Easby, much at Sedbergh and Garsdale. Easby had Stainmore and Egglestone had much in Teesdale. This Order practised more immediate pastoral care and was interested in learning. They had schools and libraries in their chapels with a teaching monk as priest. While the Cistercians employed many of the Dalesfolk on estates, a few as lay brethren but most as wage labourers, the Premonstratensians had a much closer and more personal relation with their tenants and this, with the schools, must have had some refining influence on the people of that north-western corner of the Dales, where Celtic and Norse influence was already strong. It is possible that Dalesmen like Dawson, Sedgwick, Lupton and Otterway, and the flourishing of Sedbergh School, owe something to the cultural atmosphere fostered by the Premonstratensian monks and lingering after their disappearance in the Reformation. It may even have been some remnant of this influence that led to the emergence of the Seekers in this area and so provided the nursery ground in which the message of George Fox was able to grow and flower in the Society of Friends 'in scorn called Quakers'. It is not surprising that in the Rising of the North, after the dissolution of the monasteries, peasant support was stronger in this north-western corner than in most other parts of the Dales. The charities, hospitality and sundry benefits conferred by the monasteries were well remembered.

All the monastic orders shared an interest in trade, not only local but in part international. Their early ascetic way of life had been abandoned by the officials for richer living with exotic foods, wines and fine raiment in the house of the abbot or prior. The change owed something to the increasing number of corrodians, wealthy people who exchanged their wealth for permanent residence as guests of the monastery, with little reduction in their standard of living, and assurance for their life after death. Even the smaller communities made considerable imports of wines and other expensive commodities.

The chief source of monastic income, particularly among the Cistercians, was their wool crop, which was sold to merchants from Lombardy. As the monasteries got into debt through their extravagant building programmes, they began not only to mortgage property but to make advance sales of their wool not yet grown. Members of the Italian merchant families of Florence and Venice, such as the Frescobaldi and Bernardi, themselves dressed to show off their wealth and importance and with a train of servants, came to this country to make sure of their crops. With the Cellarer of the appropriate abbey, they visited the flocks and farms taking note of conditions so as to make a reasonable assessment of the wool to be expected and its quality. The Cellarer wore his fine official robes to emphasize the importance of his abbey, had many servants, and all ceremony was observed throughout the visit. Tenants would be greatly interested and entertained with the sight of live foreign merchants and would be free of the fears that such a visit by the feudal overlord might have aroused; but at the same time the expense that they had to bear kept them in extreme poverty.

Under the monastic rule much forest was cleared, marshes drained and roads improved, and all this was accompanied by a sense of spiritual and secular security. This was a period when Dalesmen of many stocks and origins were integrated and well on the way to becoming Yorkshire Dalesmen. None the less it was also a time of strife. There were destructive raids by the Scots in the fourteenth century and the effects of the Black Death on the working population were devastating. Life in the monasteries was not all peaceful. There was much jealousy between those with adjoining estates as well as disagreements with some of the landed gentry. Some quarrels led to brawling between tenants of the differing houses, and even went as far as armed affrays. A frequent cause of strife was connected with the many water cornmills built on the estates. A mill was generally served by the damming of the stream on whose bank it stood; but in most streams the centre-line was the boundary between the estates on opposite banks. At Richmond a mill on the north bank built its dam across the stream and of course half of it trespassed on the land of a different community. A logical but unwise response was for the objector to remove the offending half of the dam, with disaster for the mill. Mills provided other pretexts for quarrels including the enticement of customers from one mill to another. Chancery and Court of Exchequer records are at no time clear of such quarrels. In all of them the tenants were involved and suffered the most. In Craven some local squires at odds with the monastery created riots and, as part of their policy of annoyance, cited the abbot of Fountains in a Craven court so that he, an old man, had to travel time after time to appear in person. The cases amount not to a few but to many dozens, and on some of them no doubt much local friction was aroused.

Widening Horizons

Henry VIII's Dissolution of the Monasteries in 1536 was not a sudden event: its coming had been foreseen and some of the more worldly-wise of the monastic officials had time to seek out and purchase small estates to which they could retire. All the monastic community, monks, nuns, abbots, priors and officials received generous pensions and many monks were appointed as vicars or rectors to churches that they had served when these had been held by the monastery. The tenants of monastic property did not fare so well. The estates were sold off at what were bargain prices to merchants of the City of London and to some of the local gentry and titled baronage, who only rarely continued to employ the army of lay servants that most monasteries had supported. Some of those displaced found occupation on the land, but many joined the 'sturdy beggars' who were everywhere increasing in number and who had previously been fed in part by the doles distributed daily at the monastery gate. The change from the known community to the unknown purchaser as landlord was resented and in the north, where the monastery/tenant relationship had in general been closer and warmer than in the south, the Dalesfolk were generally ready to support those gentry who attempted by armed riot to re-establish some of the monks in their homes.

This 'Pilgrimage of Grace' was halted and defeated at Doncaster and its leader, Aske, was executed at York. The abbots of Jervaulx, Fountains and Bridlington were also executed, all of them being well-known and respected landlords over a wide area of the Dales. Their deaths caused consternation and bitter resentment. Most of the purchasers of the monastic estates were speculators who resold them with all the tenants in them. Rents were racked and personal contacts replaced by those with a business agent. Some estates were retained by the Crown but these, like the speculators' estates, were eventually sold when the kings were in need of money. In a few fortunate places they were sold either to sitting tenants or to the freeholders who had secured leases. Kettlewell was sold by King Charles in 1628 to four Citizens of London, and they sold it to four other Citizens who, by an Act of Common Council of the Mayor, Aldermen and Commoners of the City, sold all the lordship of Kettlewell to eight local yeomen as Trustees. As time went on the Trustees sold all the houses and tenements to their occupants. Ten new freeholders were then, and ten still are, elected by the freeholders to be the Trust Lords to hold all the manorial rights and privileges in trust for the freeholders of the township. Other townships secured, through purchases and other means, the transfer of these rights to the freeholders. Conistone is held by all its freeholders, as are Hebden, Bainbridge, Woodhall, Garsdale and others. Askrigg has its group of Four Wise Men, and Dent, which from 1629 to 1670 was a Crown Manor but held in freehold tenures, in 1670 co-opted (not elected) the Twenty Sidesmen, who took over the manorial duties and rights on behalf of all the freeholders of the township. All these arrangements increased the strong element of independence in the Dales character and hastened what almost amounted to a revolution in the life and appearance of the Dales.

The Highway Acts of Henry VIII in 1530, which among other provisions ordered a survey of bridges and their subsequent repair or replacement in stone, found work for masons, masons' labourers and quarrymen left unemployed by the ending of monastic building. Before the end of the century the newly emerging class of yeomen began to think of new houses for themselves, and the gangs of masons turned from building bridges, churches and country houses to the yeoman's house as a profitable source of employment. A revolution in building was initiated, which during the following century and a half was to transform the appearance of our villages, bringing to them that core of stone buildings now so much admired.

Naturally a new house would be expected, at least by the yeoman's wife, to be in the new fashion of the times — the Tudor: sturdy, unpretentious, with stout walls, mullioned windows, stone roof and a functional plan that, in the main, adhered to the well-proven three or four-bay plan of the crucked timber house. Old habits, particularly those that make for easy working, have a power of persistence, so it should cause no surprise that some of our Dalesmen were not too proud, when planning a house for themselves, to remember the stock that quietly provided some of their prosperity. Following tradition they sometimes extended the shelter of their roof to be shared by their cattle. The Tudor 'long house' of the Dales is architecturally almost unique. It is a tribute to our Pennine weather that beside the living-room fireplace of many a long house there is a doorway onto the foddergang of the laithe. Farmers and cattle are in friendly occupation of the two sections of one building. As a boy often staying on my great-uncle's farm, a typical long house of 1630, I used to thrill towards the end of tea (afternoon drinking) to the gentle lowing of cows, the signal for my cousins to put on caps and aprons and, with me following, go through this door to fodder and milk the cows. It was a step into a world of sweet sounds and scents, crowned by a mug of milk straight from the cow. Any long house now brings to life memories precious beyond any forgetting.

While the prosperous yeomen were employing masons to provide their new houses, a few of their labourers managed by their own labour to replace their crucked wattle and thatch hovel with a modest stone cottage of no greater dimensions. Folk Museums have preserved a few early crucked cottages, and a few larger crucked barns still exist on farms in the Dales, but it is in nooks and corners of our villages that some of these 'home-made' two-roomed cottages are occasionally to be seen. So from the beginning of the seventeenth century, the villages grew into stone. The abundance of good building stones in the middle and upper Carboniferous series has made this possible, and included among them are the fine flaggy beds that provide the almost universal 'gray slate' of the stone roofs, which besides durability have a high aesthetic value.

The Reformation had been a gradual growth. Challenges to the Church had arisen two and a half centuries before the Dissolution of the Monasteries, culminating in the emergence of the group of thinkers called the Lollards, at first associated with Oxford University. As part of a complex body of new thinking they claimed that the Grace of God was dominant above all earthly authority of Pope and priest, and that God's law was given in the Bible to guide His people. It followed that for their guidance all people should be enabled to read the Bible in their own language. One of the great figures among the Lollards was a Dalesman, John Wycliffe, born at Hipswell in Swaledale in or around 1325.

Wycliffe, like some other Dales boys, proved a good scholar and was able to go to Oxford, where after graduation he settled as a tutor in the University. He became a famous scholar and in time Master of Balliol. He was deeply concerned for the reform of the University and of the Church, and became the inspiration of the Lollards. He was described as a power in the University, frail in body but of quick temper, immense energy, immovable convictions and incomparable pride, qualities that we can recognise in many Dalesmen. Of all his amazing achievements for the Lollards and for the University, his greatest may be his translation of the Bible into English between 1380 and 1384. This and his abundant tracts could of course only exist in manuscript, but many copies were made and were widely read. As the reading of the Bible in English was forbidden by the Church, Wycliffe was brought to trial; but dying in December 1384 he escaped the persecution under which many of his fellow Lollards suffered.

For a century and a half Wycliffe's Bible was read only in secret, but in the early years of the sixteenth century another Oxford scholar, William Tyndale, moved to Cambridge and came under the spell of the Greek New Testament edited by Erasmus. He was moved to say that all men should be able to know and study this book in their own language and he promised 'if God spare my life, ere many years I will cause a boy that driveth the plough shall know more of the scripture than thou dost'. In 1526 he completed a translation of the New Testament into English. It was printed in

Germany, whence six thousand copies were brought into England. As it was accompanied by many Lutheran tracts it was proscribed by the Church as Lutheran propoganda, and as many copies as could be seized were publicly burned in St Paul's Churchyard. Nevertheless more were smuggled in and were widely distributed among the poor, working people, artisans and traders.

A second Dalesman, Miles Coverdale, continues the story of the English Bible. His birth, in 1488, is reputed to have been at Coverham in Wensleydale. He was said to have been 'given to learning' as a child and in due course he went to Cambridge, being ordained priest in 1514. As the Reformation gathered way the Church Convocation asked for an English Bible. Coverdale made a translation of both Old and New Testaments, and as he was abroad at the time, this was printed and published on the Continent; but more than one edition followed in England, and in 1539 Coverdale's revision of his original, which became known as the Great Bible, was ordered to be placed in every church and to be read during the services. It might also be so placed that people could read it at other times. It was reported from many parts of the country that groups of peasants and workpeople gathered at the churches to hear the Bible read in their own language by one of themselves who could read. Coverdale's translation is in the plain English of the people, and in parts savours of his Dales origin; many phrases would have a homely flavour for northern people. In the story of the Flood the dove sent out from the Ark returned 'and she bare the olive leaf in her neb'. When Abimelech was killed with a piece of millstone it 'brake his brain pan'.

The desire to read the Bible stimulated a widespread effort by ordinary people to learn to read. Many priests responded by teaching small groups, particularly children, some in the church and some in the parsonage, and some parish clerks became noted in the registers as schoolmasters. Evening groups of adults were taught as well as day groups of children, so that by the end of the sixteenth century there was among labouring people a leavening of those who could read the Bible for themselves and to some of their neighbours. The printers responded with many editions and by the early years of the seventeenth century, the Bible was indeed becoming what Bunyan later called it, 'the book of the people'. The Protestants took their inspiration from it and the whole Protestant revolution was based upon it.

In some places those who had learned to read were starting what in the next century were to be dubbed 'dames' schools', but the main educational advance was in the founding of grammar schools. These were of various types and of many differing foundations. The chantries, founded to maintain a priest to say constant prayers for the souls of benefactors and of their kindred, were dissolved with the monasteries, but fortunately some of their endowments escaped the king's clutches and were devoted to the promotion of schools. Some of the grammar schools were of this old foundation, and after the Reformation some received substantial endowment by yeomen or merchants who had prospered. In these endowments it was frequently the custom to provide for the education of a number of poor scholars and to establish scholarships tenable at some college at Oxford or Cambridge. This provision enabled a stream of Dalesmen to attain high position in the Church or in the professional and academic worlds. A few of the grammar schools had a different origin. Dent Grammar School, for example, was founded by the Twenty Sidesmen on the subscriptions of the freeholders and people of Dent, so that it was indeed the people's own school.

The urge for education was strong enough for many of the larger villages — or for two or three in combination — to form their own school of humbler type. The net effect of all this was a fairly wide spread of literacy, which now began to characterise the yeoman class in the Dales. At first the Bible was almost the unique text-book outside the grammar schools, but by the seventeenth century a measure of numeracy was to be found in the village schools. As people began to acquire the freehold of their property or to take leases, fewer documents were accepted on a lawyer's reading and signed with a mark; full signatures became common. Miners in particular learned to read the leases of their working places, to reckon and record production and royalty charges, and to make out and understand the accounts for materials. The number of detailed mining accounts that survive from the early seventeenth century, drawn up not by an accountant, but by the working miner, is vast. In another connection, a surprising number of the first Quakers from the mid-seventeenth century onward — and most of them were drawn from the farmers and artisans — wrote and read 'epistles'; long letters were sent to justices and others in authority and many journals were written and published. With all this the Bible and, later, Bunyan's *Pilgrim's Progress* remained the two books to be found in most Dales homes except the poorest. Many of the Bibles were supplied by the fourth Lord Wharton's charity which, originating among his miners in Swaledale, has continued from the last decades of the seventeenth century until now.

In the nineteenth century the Mechanic's Institutes, founded by George Birkbeck of the Quaker family of Settle, were established in many of the Dales villages and most of them had extensive and well used libraries of scientific and technical works, as well as serious books of standard literature and philosophy. These libraries were used especially by the miners, and education was more widely spread by lectures arranged by 'the Mechanics' as the Institutes were familarly known. These were often given by men of the standard of Thomas Huxley. The opportunity for education was also extended by Nonconformist chapels, many of which had small libraries in their Sunday Schools that at least encouraged, with books carefully chosen, the habit of reading. Many fostered small societies, guilds, lecture groups, young Men's Associations and similar bodies that all encouraged debate and thinking.

By the mid-seventeenth century a new network of tracks and green ways was being laid down over the country, but these had a north to south directional pattern. Along these tracks armies of cattle were drained from Scotland to feed the hungry south. A new race of men, the drovers, led cattle in groups numbering from tens to hundreds of animals, to 'gatherings' mostly on the high moors or on commons, for only there could room be found for them to rest overnight or be assembled for sale. Many were bought by Dales farms and overwintered there to feed them up for the butchers or for the further journey south. So drovers, boys, dogs and cattle, with a donkey or two to carry food and a few other necessities, joined the moorland pageant. The gatherings were frequent through a long season each year and the numbers of cattle suprisingly large. At Great Close on Malham Moor one dealer with his many drovers in one year brought ten thousand cattle from the Highlands. The season's total was frequently more than twenty thousand, and Great Close was only one of the many gatherings within the periphery of the Dales. We can say that in the height of the two centuries during which this trade lasted, cattle in numbers in excess of a hundred thousand were driven each year across the Dales and over the high-level tracks, where now the shepherd is almost the only user of them.

There were other travellers on the moorland ways, particularly in the nineteenth century and so within the memory of recent generations. These were the wool men, or 'broggers', who took out wool from markets like Halifax to be spun in Dales farmhouses and homes, and then collected the spun yarn to take back to market or mill. A group special to the northern dales were the distributors of knitting wool and the collectors of the caps, gloves and stockings knitted by the Dales people. Almost everyone knitted, men, women and children, whenever they could. Knitting was often the occupation of a social evening gathering. Other users of the pack roads were pedlars travelling on regular rounds with drapery and small goods, and often called 'Scotsmen', and this so late that as a boy I knew one well and often listened to his tales. The pack-horse tracks were often named: in Dentdale there are the Galloway Gate and the Driving Road, which cross the moors to Garsdale and further. Swaledale, like many other parts of the Dales, has its Jagger Road and Jagger Lane, and names like Load Saddle Hill and Slippery Ford mark the descents to streams to be crossed. 'Badger Gate', 'Limers Way' and 'Salters Gate' indicate the special users of these tracks.

All along the drove roads, inns sprang up almost solely for the use of the drovers, although a few, like Gearstones, or Spital on Stainmore are documented as far back as monastic times. Many of these old places, away on the moors where the droving tracks converge, can still be found if only as heaps of rubble or sparse foundations, unnoticed and forgotten like Great Close on Malham Moor or the Waste Inn on Boss Moor. A few like Tan Hill were preserved by a later use, Tan Hill being in the midst of old collieries and for a time the calling place for the drovers who carried the coal to farms all over the adjacent dales. Tan Hill also had a small sheep fair that still meets. Gearstones Inn at Ribblehead still, after the droving was ended, kept a small market fostered by the great complex of drove roads that met there.

My maternal grandmother, born in Wensleydale in 1840, was seventy when as a boy of fourteen I gathered family history and Dales lore from her at every opportunity. She was proud that as a girl of eight she regularly rode pillion behind her father to market. Sometimes they went to Gearstones. After hay harvest, accompanied by a boy with a donkey, they took a load of cheeses made by her mother and two aunts, all noted cheese-makers: these were sold and a winter stock of oatmeal brought back. She married Michael Bell from Swaledale, whose grandfather had often told him tales of an ancestor who in the seventeenth century was a drover of cattle from Sutherland, came to fairs in Yorkshire, and there married a Swaledale girl and settled down. My grandmother knew other families with drover connections, and one might ask if the Sutherland drovers felt some kinship with Dalesfolk, as both had been subject to Norse settlement in the remote past.

Industrial Revolution

During the eighteenth and nineteenth centuries the Dalesfolk could be thought of as belonging to two very distinct groups, sometimes one and sometimes the other making up the largest part of the labouring population. Farmers and landworkers were the one and miners and quarrymen the other. Each group of course employed anciliary craftsmen, blacksmiths and carriers being used by both. The prime differences that affected outlook and character were many and strongly marked. The farmer spent most of the daylight hours in the open air, subject to and dependent upon the weather, which despite its vagaries and occasional storms was his friend. It was closely watched, studied with skill, and dictated the first greeting when people met. The farmer's prime resource was the soil, and soil and weather together gave him his crops and his livelihood. He was a breeder and keeper of animals, in turn dependent on the product of the soil for their food, and his invariable friend and his assistant was his dog. Most of his animals were dependent upon his care at their birth and during their upbringing, and to be successful with them he needed to be gentle and ever attentive. His life and work were directed to providing food for himself and the community, his operations were all concerned with living things and all life's processes, and his routine was set by the seasons.

Most aspects of the miner's life were the opposite of this. His was a complex operation, winning metals from the earth, wrestling always with dead, insensitive rock that could be hammered with pick and blown up with gunpowder. His strength was regularly taxed to the limit. More than one process was needed before metal was got, the miner getting 'bouse' (a mixture of ore and rock) from the ground, the dresser washing and cleaning ore from impurities, and the smelter with his furnaces finally separating the metal. Each had their different environment for work. The dresser was the one who, like the farmer, was out of doors, but he worked on an open site in one place, always exposed to wind and weather, mixing and treating his bouse with running water in great quantities. Women were often employed in this capacity, and some thoughtful employers would provide them with heavy woollen skirts; but it is doubtful how much comfort these would give when saturated. The smelter was under cover but facing great heat from his open furnace and with back exposed to draughts and cold; what with fume from the lead (most of the mines were lead mines), he was usually not a robust man but subject to consumptions and lead poisoning.

The miner, with very occasional exceptions, spent all his working time underground in a world of near darkness, with one small tallow candle, not always a sufficiency of air, dust from his rock cutting, fumes from the frequent blasting and always plenty of wet. He often walked two or three miles from his home to the remote mine where he worked, situated far up in the hills. For part of the year this walk was made in the dark before dawn, and he likewise returned in the dark of early night. In the summer months he might enjoy the dawn chorus of the birds and see the first stirrings of nature to the new day. For part of the year he would be coming home in the twilight, 'owl light', and could see the hunting owls and buzzards and perhaps see and hear the bats. A slinking fox was no uncommon sight, and a hare or rabbit could with skill be made a welcome addition to the pot. Despite the dark, tracks almost invisible to a casual visitor took him in instinctive safety past bog holes and old shafts. Most miners had the habit of singing along their journeys, a habit based on a reasonable belief that the extra breathing of pure moorland air was a healthy antidote to the foul air of the mine. Generally it was hymns that were sung, with gusto, and they not only lightened the way but gave some protection against Barguest, Peg Nell, Jack o' Lanterns and other undesirable companions.

The miner's place of work was, more often than not, narrow, with little room for two men at most, foul-smelling with sweat, tallow stithe and powder fume. Once or twice in a shift, blasts were fired to bring down the rock, and for a time refuge was taken round some convenient bend of the workings. To counter the effects of bad air the London Lead Company and later the Beaumont Company provided allotments and even smallholdings for some miners. The bargain system allowed him to arrange his working times and, with the help of his family, he could manage a small hay-meadow, a cow, pig and poultry, and perhaps a sheep or two. In this way his health was considerably improved as well as his diet. The psychological effect was also very beneficial, though a few employers said that it made the miner too independent. The holding corrected his lack of contact with living things and provided a common interest between him and the farmer. The benefit was not only to the individual but to relations within the village community.

The miner works for the discovery and extraction of ores that are unseen until gotten and are everywhere uncertain and variable in their occurrence. He must exercise a high degree of observation, experience and skill to recognise evidence that might lead him to ore. He must learn the nature and properties of the rocks in which he is working, and above all he must have faith and patience. Making a level to approach a vein or to drain a mine involves driving through dead rock, investing labour against future gains. There are levels that have taken thirty years to drive before any benefit was got from them. The farmer looks every year for his harvest both of crops and of animals and will be sure of them, good or bad. There is no such certainty in mining.

When Wesley came to the Dales in 1777 he was not at first accepted, but his vigorous faith in salvation, in a certain future, and in the triumph of a spiritual life that was the antithesis of this world, had a special appeal for the miners. When they took up Wesley's message, it was whole-heartedly and with great enthusiasm. In most mining villages, after meetings had been held for some time in houses, chapels were built, often by the miners' own hands. Working in stone was natural to them, and their skill in walling and arching, inside the mine levels, helped them to build in a substantial fashion that has lasted at least two centuries. The little unadorned, functional Bethels and Zions had little beauty and by some modern scoffers have been called 'God boxes', but nonetheless they were places of ecstatic spiritual experience. The miners' musical skills and habits brought into the chapels a tradition of robust singing such that former generations have testified that it was there they 'first glimpsed heaven and heard the angels sing'.

A feature of Methodism was an extensive system of local preachers upon which most of the small chapels depended. The voluntary preachers were 'planned' to serve small chapels in turn, often at some distance from their home. The zealous 'locals' would regularly walk miles to a chapel to take services for a day, often setting off in early morning and returning during part of the night, possibly crossing from one dale to the next over the moors. As this was the regular pattern for many miners going to their work, and as farmers were more tied by the care of their animals and seldom had occasion to leave their own land and sheep-run, it was the miners who formed a large part of the preachers' 'plan'. The gospel they preached was robust, their delivery vigorous and homely. On their long walks to and from work they had time to ponder their next sermon and it was usually of strong stuff. Direct and vivid illustration was not uncommon. One well-known 'local' liked to show the ease of the way to Hell by sliding down the rail of the pulpit steps, and would then illustrate the climb back to Heaven by a struggle up the rail watched by all with held breath. 'Heaven' was not always regained. A stirring sermon might be interrupted by shouts of Glory, Praise Be, Halleluiah. Some preachers were known to be 'exhorters' who at a prayer meeting could fill the penitents' form and who were specially welcome at the Love Feasts, somewhat the equivalent of church Communion. The chapel was also the centre of social life for its congregation and was frequently the home of a Sunday School and a Band of Hope.

The miners' habit of singing as they walked to and from their work was paralleled by

opportunities. They created new demands for catering and accommodation, and introduced some urbanisation of ideas. They were a foretaste of the invasion that was to accompany the development of the motor car.

The Spirit of the Dales

The long story of man's life in the Dales has revealed the steady evolution of a community with some features in the character of its people and in their dialect, that mark them as worthy of a distinctive and descriptive name. To call a man a Dalesman (remembering that the title is bi-sexual and includes Daleswoman) implies not only his origin, upbringing and immediate environment within the Pennine dales, but imputes to him some recognisable habits of life and thought. The Pennines are a large area and it is possible to distinguish the people of the Yorkshire Dales from those of Durham or Derbyshire by some traits in their character and in their folk speech and folk lore, as well as in their geographical location and their history. Without pursuing these distinctions we may ask what are the particular qualities that go to make up the Yorkshire Dalesman.

The dialect that he speaks is properly a matter for the etymologist and the grammarian; suffice it to say that the Norse invaders who left us a rich vocabulary were far more numerous in the mid-Pennine Dales than they were either to north or south, and their enrichment of the local speech is strongly evident in both dialect and place-names. The rough topography, the hard climate and the virtual isolation from the outside world through many centuries are shared by all the dales and have contributed to the breeding of a basic Pennine character; but the thin and scattered nature of much of the population that lies between the two great cross routes of the Aire Gap and Stainmore, the likelihood of being quite cut off in winter storms and floods, the prevalence of high ground and the general difficulty of communication between one dale and the next, have bred a people among whom an almost aggressive self-sufficiency and independence are expected and valued qualities.

A person lacking these qualities is said to be 'slack set up', 'slammoky' or would by my grandmother have been described as 'summat an nowt, wants a nurse, shoo does'. There are a score of other terms for such persons. This self-reliance does nothing to reduce the instant and unstinted help given quietly, efficiently and without fuss in any emergency as soon as it is known. Dalesfolk are afraid of fuss and distrust it. They are slow-spoken, given to hiding their emotions and always wedded to understatement. A man in robust health would be most likely to say he 'wor noan so bad' and that might also be his verdict on his wife's special effort in cookery, he feeling that he had given high praise. 'I'm nobbut middling' or 'I'm raither poorly' could be the reply of a person very ill or not far from death. One might hope to detect no more than a proper avoidance of over-praise when, after critical and weighty consideration, it is said of a piece of work that 'it mud (might) a been warr (worse)'; and an emotional parting is sometimes avoided with 'Nah, tak care o' thysen, owd lad'. This use of 'owd lad' or 'lad' is properly a mark of affection widely and sincerely bestowed between friends, and has little reference to age. It would not be used to describe a person but only in address to one.

The Dalesman has a deep and often partly concealed sense of humour, frequently with a grim turn or touched with something of the macabre. His quick wit in repartee has the same flavour. All this is a reflection of the age-old struggle against a tough environment in which living means constant effort. He is a hard bargainer and is careful, even 'near', in money matters, but again this is a product of making a living that is possible only by hard work and constant watchfulness amid conditions that often appear adverse. The true Dalesman has integrity and, like Wycliffe, holds his 'unswerving convictions', often mistakenly described as obstinacy by those who know him least well. Withal, he has generosity and a great impulse to hospitality. These qualities are blended with an intense local pride and love and loyalty to his dale, never flaunted but always there, a part of his nature.

In recent decades this distinctive character has been challenged, for it is being subjected to considerable pressure by the impact of a different culture. It is a multi-headed attack. The popularity of the motor car has brought thousands of townspeople into the Dales, visitors, mostly for a few hours only, attracted by the scenery so well advertised by the travel agents. Quiet villages win admiration and by their admirers are made unquiet. Car drivers enjoy exploring narrow by-roads and soon create the conditions that call for their widening. There is also increasing demand for weekend and holiday cottages, and now in summer whenever the weather is good there is an invasion vastly greater than any previously experienced in the history of the Dales. Like their predecessors, these invaders bring with them an alien culture — this time an urban one; and this the media supplement with their popularisation of habits and tastes imported from the wider world. How are the Dales and their communities reacting to this last invasion? How can they still preserve the things that have attracted the invaders — unspoiled natural scenery, undisturbed villages and a highly individual way of life created by many centuries of slow evolution?

Dalesfolk live in the valleys but look to the hills — the hills that are always there, symbols of stability and permanence, not changing noticeably within a long human life. On the hills, quiet and healing solitude can be found after the exertion of the climb. Among those of the Dales population who will accept and serve the expanding demands of the invaders, there is a growing nucleus of those who will fight to preserve the qualities of their rural way of life that have matured through many centuries, are rooted in the Dales environment, and strongly ingrained in the people through many generations.

The physical Dales may be scarred by quarries and blanketed in parts by monotonous plantations of conifers, made noisy by busy roads and crowded car parks, but they are large enough to bear these scars even as they regret them. Some of the Dalesfolk both old and young will still look to and go to the hills. They will seek rest and quiet contemplation, as they absorb the broad spread of the country they love. They will gather peace and refreshment of body, mind and spirit. This section of the 'native' Dalesfolk will meet all the challenges and changes that are bound to come, and there is increasing evidence that their love of the Dales is as great as that which Dalesmen have held in the past. They will, like their forebears, hesitate to speak of and define the Spirit of the Dales, but they will live in it and it will be preserved to serve and inspire future generations, as it has been the inspiring force in the past. May it be so.

THE PHOTOGRAPHS

Barbondale — looking along the line of the Dent Fault

East Gill Foss at Kisdon, Swaledale

Chapel-le-Dale with its glaciated limestone scars

Dent Head Viaduct and Dentdale

Langstrothdale — upper Wharfedale

A drove-road on Combe Fell

Kitty Gill bringing in the 'eldin'

Erosion channels in Coverdale

The River Dee

Pendragon Castle and Wild Boar Fell

Swaledale from the Buttertubs Pass

Thwaite, Swaledale — a Norse settlement

Jim and Ivy Mason from Barras House, Gawthrop

Herbert and Ennis Bentham on their way to mark the tup

Scotchergill Farm

Jim Taylor taking his cows to be milked

Alan Mattinson converts a Dales barn

Mily Taylor and John Murdoch at dominoes in the Sun Inn, Dent

Main Street, Dent

Ingleborough and limestone pavement

The Main Chamber of Gaping Gill — Britain's largest known cavern

Herb Robert growing on a stone wall

The Buttertubs

Old Cote Moor across Littondale

Feeding Swaledale sheep above Artengill Viaduct

Askrigg Village and Addleborough

Denys Stark, the proprietor

Ivy Bentham, East Banks Farm

A Long House near Appersett

Ingleton Quarry — working in Yorkshire's oldest rock

Pete Moorby and Jo Hartley repair the Chapel roof using stone slates

Shaw Beck — remains of a lead-mining hamlet

Elizabeth and Thomas Gardner at Banklands Farm

Dent Village under Rise Hill

Deepdale Beck at Mill Bridge

Ted Sedgwick from New Closes, Cowgill

The Howgill Fells from Deepdale

A traditional hay meadow in Swaledale

Getting the hay in — Deepdale

Robert Mason rounding up the tups with his dog 'Leo'

Tug of war — Gala Day

Malham Cove

Malham Tarn with Great Crested Grebe

The Shores of Malham Tarn, with alder, birch and 'bog baby warning'

Watlowes at Malham — a dry valley

Alum Pot as seen from the Long Churn Cave System

Grotto in Gavel Pot

Ribblehead Viaduct and Batty Moss

Aysgarth — The Middle Falls

'Tizza' Middleton

Wood Anemones in a gryke

Lockingarth Falls, Deepdale

Icicle detail

Jo and Phyllis Woof dipping sheep at Cautley

A pack-horse track cuts across Greenhow Hill

Hubberholme Church

School children — West Burton

Tommy Capstick and Harold Goad having a 'biting on'

Colt Park — relict ash-wood

Janet's Foss — The Fairy's Cave

The Roof Tunnel in Kingsdale Master Cave

Yew Cogar Scars rise sharply above Cowside Beck

A cascade on Deepdale Beck cuts through the Yoredale Strata

Main Stream Passage, Lancaster Hole

Swaledale

Mist rising from the Keld

'Topping' a wall in Kingsdale

Richard Charnley at Hawes Market

Brushing the sheeps' faces ready for the Mule Gimmer Sale

Beth of Dent

Formations in Cross Fell Cave

Gordale Scar

Gordale Beck — downstream from Janet's Foss

Jervaulx Abbey

Jervaulx Abbey — detail of one of its numerous stone arches

Alum Pot 240 ' below the surface

Dentdale and Middleton Fell

Martin Cragg with the muck-spreader

Ben Munro's Bicycle Shop

Mr and Mrs Baines at Backstone Gill, Dentdale

Douglas Hartley catching the wayward lamb

Pen-y-ghent — early morning

Willie Bentham

INDEX

Abbotside 35
Addingham 27
Addlebrough 17/26
Aire (river) 14/21/27
Airedale 22/25/28/29/33/35/43
Aire Gap 44
Aire Head Springs 16
Aisgill 21
Aldborough 26
Almondbury 25
Alston Block 14
Alston Moor 14
Appletreewick 34
Arcow Wood 13
Arkengarthdale 31/32
Armley 28
Arncliffe 26
Askrigg 31/32/35/36
Askrigg Block 14/15/21
Attermire 23
Aysgarth 21/24
Badger Gate 39
Bainbridge 26/32/36
Bardale 32
Barden Scale 30
Baugh Fell 22
Bedale 43
Bolton Priory 35
Boroughbridge 25/26
Borrowdale 34
Bowland 30
Boss Moor 39
Bradley 28
Bridlington Priory 35/36
Buckden 32
Buckden Pike 15
Buck Haw Brow 14
Burnley 43
Burnsall-with-Thorpe 29
Burtersett 30
Byland Abbey 35
Calder (river) 25/27/33
Carperby 17
Carpley Green 26/32
Castle Dykes 24
Catterick 28/31
Cautley Scar 19
Clapham Beck Head 16
Clough (river) 11, 21
Colne 25
Colt Park Wood 20
Combe Scar 19
Conistone 34/36
Cotterdale 17
Countersett 30/32
Coverham 35/38
Cowling 27
Craven 14/15/19/23/36
Crummackdale 13
Dearne (river) 21
Dee (river) 11, 21
Dent 31/36/38
Dentdale 11/19/22/29/30/39
Devil's Arrows 25
Dibb (river) 34
Don (river) 21
Driving Road 39
Easby 35
Ease Gill Cave System 16
Easter Grotto 16
Eden (river) 21
Eden (Vale of) 14
Egglestone Abbey 35
Elmet 27
Escrick 25
Fell Beck 15
Fors 31
Fountains Abbey 34/36

Fountains Fell 15
Fremington Dykes 26
Furness Abbey 34
Galloway Gate 39
Gaping Gill 15/16
Garsdale 11/22/29/30/35/36/39/43
Gearstones 39/40
Gilling 31
Gordale Scar 14
Grassington 22/24/26
Great Close 39
Great Close Tarn 23
Great Shunner Fell 17
Great Whernside 15
Gregory 26
Grewelthorpe 19
Grinton 22/32
Gunnerside 30
Halifax 39
Hardrow 21
Harkerside 20
Hawes 43
Healaugh 20/32
Hebden 36
Hellifield 43
Hexham 28
High Force 20
High Raise 32
Hipswell 37
Horton 32/34
Howgills 13/14/19
Hubberholme 31
Huddersfield 25
Humber (river) 11/21/25
Ilkley 28
Ingleborough 15/16/18/20/26/34
Ingleton 13
Jagger Lane 39
Jagger Road 39
Jervaulx 35/36
Kettlewell 32/35/36
Kilnsey 26/34
Kilnsey Crag 21
Kirkby Lonsdale 11/29
Kirkby Stephen 11/29
Kirkdale Cave 22
Kisdon Hill 21
Kisdon (ravine) 21
Knaresborough 21/30
Lancaster Hole 16
Langcliffe 19
Langstrothdale 30/31
Lea Green 26
Leeds 28
Leyburn 43
Limers Way 39
Lindisfarne 28
Linton 22
Litton 30/31/32
Load Saddle Hill 39
Lothersdale 22
Lovely Seat 15/18
Lunds Fell 21
Lune (Vale of) 43
Lunersett 18
Malham 16/19/26/34/35
Malham Cove 14
Malham Moor 35/39
Malham Tarn 16/23
Mallerstang 21/22/29
Marsett 32
Marwood 31
Mastiles Lane 34
Mewith 31/32
Mickle Fell 20
Middleham 31
Middle Tongue 15
Moughton 20

Nelson 43
Netherside 21
New Forest 30/32
Nidd (river) 21/22
Nidderdale 35/43
Norber 19
Northallerton 43
Otley 28
Ouse (river) 11/21
Outgang 26
Pateley Bridge 11
Pendle 18
Penhill 17/18/32
Pen-y-ghent 15/16/18
Prior's Rake 35
Ravenseat 30
Rawthey (river) 11/14
Raydale 32
Reeth 31/32
Ribble (river) 21/22/34
Ribblehead 29/34/39
Ribblesdale 13/19/31/35/43
Richmond 11/21/22/26/31/35/43
Ripon 28/29
Rogan's Seat 17/18
Rombalds Moor 25
Salters Gate 39
Samson's Toe 19
Sawley Abbey 35
Scarborough 23/25
Sedbergh 35
Semer Water 32
Settle 22/31/39/43
Shunner Fell 17/18
Simon Fell 18
Skeb Skeugh 21
Skipton 11/22/28/31/35
Skirethorns Cave 23
Slippery Ford 39
Southerscales 26/30
Spital 39
Stainforth 35
Stainmore 14/35/39/44
Stake Pass 26
Stang 15
Stanwick 18/26
Star Carr 23
Stridebuts 26
Swale (river) 20/21/22/28/29/31
Swaledale
22/26/29/30/31/32/33/35/37/39/40/43
Ta Dyke 26
Tan Hill 39
Tees (river) 21/31
Teesdale 14/20/35/43
Thornber 26
Thornborough Moor 24
Thornton Force 13
Threshfield 34
Thwaite 30
Tyne (river) 14
Ure (river) 13/17/21/22/29/33/43
Victoria Cave 22/23
Waldendale 17
Waste Inn 39
Water Crag 15/17
Water Sinks 16
Weardale 14
Wensleydale
11/13/17/21/22/26/30/31/32/35/38/39/42
Wharfe (river) 27/34
Wharfedale 11/15/21/22/25/29/31/35/43
Whernside 15/16/18
White Birch 21
Whitby 25/28
Widdale 18/29
Wild Boar Fell 16/17/18/22
Winterburn (river) 35

Winterings 30
Winterscales 30
Woodhall 36
Yarnbury 24
Yockenthwaite 25/30
Yoredale 13/21
York 25/28/30/36
York (Vale of) 24/26/29/31